BASIC PROBLEMS OF MARX'S PHILOSOPHY

ESSAY AND MONOGRAPH SERIES

OF

THE LIBERAL ARTS PRESS

Oskar Piest, Founder

BASIC PROBLEMS OF MARX'S PHILOSOPHY

Nathan Rotenstreich

THE BOBBS-MERRILL COMPANY, INC.
PUBLISHERS • INDIANAPOLIS • NEW YORK

SECOND PRINTING

LIBRARY OF CONGRESS CATALOG CARD NUMBER 64-66073
ISBN 0-672-61210-0 (pbk)
ISBN 0-672-60163-X
PRINTED IN THE UNITED STATES OF AMERICA
DESIGNED BY JEAN KRULIS

CONTENTS

PREFACE

The interest in Karl Marx's philosophy, especially in his early writings, is growing today, and an immense literature is devoted to it. The present book, based on interpretations of the author published in both Hebrew and German, deals with principles and problems of Marx's philosophy chiefly by means of a running commentary on his "Theses on Feuerbach." The commentary is supplemented by analyses of Marx's *The Poverty of Philosophy* and the concept of alienation. The critical evaluation of Marx's theory emerges gradually in the course of the interpretation and is summed up in an analysis of the relationship between existence and consciousness.

Marx's philosophy as such was formulated in what are called his early writings. In his later writings, Marx moved toward history and economics, although he tried to integrate his former philosophical findings into his historical and economic thought.

I am grateful to Professor R. Bernstein of Yale University for his interest, and to my students, A. Gerstein and M. Kubovi, for their help in preparing the manuscript for the press.

Jerusalem, 1964 *Nathan Rotenstreich*

BASIC PROBLEMS OF MARX'S PHILOSOPHY

CHAPTER 1

Feuerbach's Shift from Theology to Anthropology

LITERARY FRAMEWORK

Karl Marx described the course of his ideological development in the introduction to his *A Contribution to the Critique of Political Economy*. At one point he says:

> Friedrich Engels, with whom I was continually corresponding and exchanging ideas . . . came by a different road to the same conclusions as myself. . . . We decided to work out together the contrast between our view and the idealism of the German philosophy, in fact to settle our accounts with our former philosophic conscience. The plan was carried out in the form of a criticism of the post-Hegelian philosophy. The manuscript in two solid octavo volumes had long reached the publisher in Westphalia, when we received information that conditions had so changed as not to allow of its publication. We abandoned the manuscript to the stinging criticism of the mice, the more readily since we had accomplished our main purpose—the clearing up of the question to ourselves.[1]

The essay to which Marx refers, "The German Ideology,"[2]

[1] Karl Marx, *A Contribution to the Critique of Political Economy*, trans. N. I. Stone from 2d German edn. (Chicago: C. H. Kerr, 1911), pp. 13–14.

[2] Karl Marx and Friedrich Engels, "Die Deutsche Ideologie," in *Karl Marx and Friedrich Engels—Historische-kritische Gesamtausgabe*, ed. Vladimir Adoradskij (Berlin, 1932); these volumes will be

remained unknown until it was published in its entirety by Rjazanov and later by Landshut and Mayer.

Friedrich Engels, Marx's collaborator and editor, referred to this same essay in the introduction to his book on Ludwig Feuerbach:

> Before sending this manuscript to press I once again hunted up and examined the old manuscript of 1845–46. The part of it dealing with Feuerbach is not complete. . . . On the other hand I have found in an old volume of Marx the eleven essays on Feuerbach. . . . These are notes hurriedly scribbled in for later elaboration, not in the least degree prepared for the press, but invaluable, as the first written form in which is planted the genial germ of the new philosophy.[3]

An attempt is made here to interpret and to explain Marx's "Theses on Feuerbach" by means of a clarification of their content, which is often only hinted at or implied. This analysis should substantiate the significance of the "Theses," because they contain the core of Marx's views and reveal the origin of his ideas that were later greatly amplified.

Engels was the first to publish Marx's "Theses on Feuerbach," and since then the custom has been to publish them in the summary of Engel's book on Feuerbach. My translation of the "Theses" is not based on the text published by Engels, however, but rather on the original text published by Rjazanov and Landshut-Mayer.[4] The latter is certainly to be preferred, for there are differences between the texts in certain, often important, details. Yet there has been no systematic research

---

referred to throughout as *MEGA*. *See also* Karl Marx, *Der historische Materialismus: die Frühschriften*, ed. S. Landshut and J. P. Mayer (Leipzig: F. Kröner, 1932).

[3] Friedrich Engels, *Feuerbach, The Roots of the Socialist Philosophy*, trans., with a critical introduction, by Austin Lewis (Chicago: C. H. Kerr, 1919), pp. 35–36. The translation is not always faithful to the German text.

[4] *See* n. 2 above.

comparing the original text to that of Engels nor a clarification of the reasons why Engels changed the original.[5]

The attempt to elucidate the philosophical principles of Marx necessitates the clarification of his early writings, those that preceded 1848. Included are numerous polemics: the essay "German Ideology," which was related to the "Theses on Feuerbach" and was itself a polemic against Feuerbach, Bruno Bauer, and Max Stirner; essays written against Hegel; the great essay "The Holy Family," directed against Stirner and Bauer, against whom the article "On the Jewish Question" was also directed. Marx's positive position was developed through this polemic, and from that point of view the "Theses on Feuerbach" stood at the crossroad. The first step here is the explanation of the polemic and its aim.

ON FEUERBACH

The death of Hegel in 1831 had manifold consequences within the history of thought and the history of society. Hegel's system had become pre-eminent in the German thought of the period. It claimed to be a self-enclosed system, embracing all human activity; yet, even in the eyes of Hegel's contemporaries, his system had begun to reveal imperfections. Those very characteristics that had seemed to indicate its strength now appeared to testify to its weakness. The thought of the period was devoted to two fundamental questions, concerned with the relationship between religion and philosophy and the relationship between reality and reason. Both questions brought to light internal conflicts that destroyed the unity of Hegel's school.

[5] This issue is mostly probably related to the differences between Marx and Engels. *See* the fundamental study of Ernst Lewalter, *Wissensoziologie und Marxismus,* eine Auseinandersetzung mit Karl Mannheims "Ideologie und Utopie" von Marxistisher Position aus, *Archiv für Sozialwissenschaft und Sozialpolitik* (Tübingen, 1930), LIV, 63 ff.

Relationship Between Religion and Philosophy. Hegel could not avoid dealing with the problem of the relationship between religion and philosophy, not only because of his theological training but also because of his principal objective, which was to include in a comprehensive system every field of human activity in its historical development as well as in its intrinsic nature. He dealt with history, law, logic, anthropology, religion, and art. Any field involving either man or Spirit—the total of men's creations and their contents—was subject matter for his system.

His basic question was: What is the particular place of religion among these spheres of human activity? What is the exact position and status of religion in Hegel's all-embracing philosophical system? Religion is a line between art and philosophy proper. Hegel's answer was not new; it is to be found in medieval thought as well. He asserted that actually there was no difference in the content of philosophy and religion, only a difference in the form and quality of the exposition of their content. Whereas religion expresses the absolute spiritual content in the language of images relating to man's world of everyday experience, philosophy expresses this self-same absolute content in the language of explicit concepts detached from everyday descriptive or metaphorical language.

Christianity represents the highest level in the development of religion, according to Hegel, manifesting both the tension and dynamics characteristic of the Spirit in the metaphorical language of Father, Son, and Holy Ghost. Philosophy, of which the mode of expression is concept proper, manifests this dynamic tension by means of another trinity, the dialectical one—thesis, antithesis, and synthesis. It can be said that Spirit, the power that directs history, replaces the will of God in Christianity, and the idea of "the cunning of reason" replaces the idea of divine providence. The cunning of reason is reason taking advantage of human passions for the sake of achieving its end, e.g., taking advantage of the lust for personal power for the sake of achieving freedom. Here a change takes place in the very form itself on which each of the two spheres depends, but the basic unity of content has not been marred. In his attempt to bridge the difference between religion and philosophy, Hegel set out to identify the exclusive place of religion in his system and to "concile"—to use his own term—the apparently distinct and opposing spheres of religion and philosophy.

Thus Hegel himself viewed philosophy as the supreme level of Spirit, its absolute summit, towering above and beyond religion. The form of philosophy—the concept—is more adequate to the spiritual content than is the form of religion—the image. Furthermore, the conceptual form is integrated and unified through and through. In the conceptual form the Spirit achieves its self-realization, and nothing exists beyond its self-awareness.

Despite their uniformity of content, the transition from religion to philosophy as Hegel saw it clearly represents progress. This necessarily anticipates a question that Hegel himself did not discuss sufficiently. Once the ultimate level of philosophy has been attained, is there still room for religion? Perhaps only an historical, relative position can be reserved for religion, which remains justified only as long as the stage of the concept has not been reached; once the level of the concept has been attained, religion becomes superfluous.

The Hegelian school split into three main branches over this question. Hegel's contemporaries understood this division as a split from the main stream of Hegelianism into small *hyparchies*. His followers were called *Diadochs,* a term used of Alexander the Great's inheritors, who divided his empire. The three branches of Hegelianism formed during those years were known as the rightists, the centrists, and the leftists. The rightists chose to maintain religion by a reversal of the conceptual refinement effected by Hegel's system into a new religious content; their main representative was the Protestant theologian Philipp Marheineke. The centrists preferred in different ways to maintain both spheres, religion and philosophy, so that the conceptual ultimateness of philosophy would not infringe on the independence of religion. They were represented mainly by Johann Erdmann. The leftists chose to infer conclusions from theory to practice within Hegel's system of taking seriously the view that genuine progress has been made in the transition from religion to philosophy; in other words, after having arrived at philosophy, they chose to reject religion.

Feuerbach himself was identified with the leftist branch of Hegelianism. Another notable leftist was Bruno Bauer, the friend during Marx's youth, from whom he disengaged himself. Marx gave the reasons for this break in two essays—"On the Jewish Question" and "The Holy Family." David Friedrich Strauss was identified also as a leftist. His work on the life of Jesus attempted to point out the legendary or mythological foundations of the Christian religion. Both Strauss and Bauer used the criterion laid down by Hegel in his theory, at least as they understood it, in examining the history of religion. The importance of Feuerbach and Marx in this development will be discussed in greater detail below.

Relationship Between Reality and Reason. Hegel, then, sought to include all areas of human activity in his theory and to understand them as different manifestations of Spirit. He claimed the system to be absolute insofar as it reserved a place for every significant occurrence and encompassed the world in one universal framework. The question that necessarily came up because of the very nature of such a theory was: What is the place and the significance of concrete reality, here and now, placed in time and space, once it has already been understood and thus included in the systematic framework? It is certain that reality still continues. The time in which we live still flows on within it. Is it possible that reality can remain independent of the self-enclosed system that understands and judges it? Is the system created to become a real force within reality or is reality designed to be an independent force outside of the system?

The Hegelian leftists based their argument on reality. Using different types and degrees of attack on the system, they claimed to demonstrate the independence and creative force of factual reality beyond the factitious system. Some argued that the rational-conceptual system developed and reached definitiveness while reality—mainly social and historical—still lagged behind it. Others completely separated the domains of reality and reason in order to demonstrate the weakness of idealistic philosophy as opposed to living reality. A man of the age, Sören Kierkegaard, gave radical expression to this prevalent feeling. But he was also disappointed by the direction speculative philosophy had taken and as a result worked out a new religious approach. He stated: "What the philosophers say about Reality is often as disapointing as a sign you see in a shop window which reads: 'Pressing Done Here.' If you brought your clothes to be pressed, you would be fooled, for the sign is only for sale." [6]

Change in Point of Departure. This background helps to explain Feuerbach's theory and the proximity of Marx's theory to it. Feuerbach also based on reality his argument against the systematic idealistic philosophy. The essence of his argument revealing the limitations of idealistic philosophy can be summarized as follows: (1) Hegel's idealistic philosophy made the real world distant and removed, a world beyond our grasp. The world that is closest, the world of concrete reality perceived empirically by the senses, is made remote. This philosophy wrongly emphasized the distance of thought from reality and the removal of reality to a position beyond concrete observation, the feature precisely important to man. (2) Because this system of thought is self-enclosed, it can actually be called a philosophy that assumes itself and lives off itself. It is meaningful only to those already well-established within it. (3) The point of departure of any idealistic philosophy is knowl-

[6] Sören Kierkegaard, *Either/Or,* I, trans. David F. Swenson and Lillian M. Swenson, with revisions and a foreword by Howard A. Johnson (Garden City, New York: Doubleday, 1959), p. 31.

edge and the consciousness linked with knowledge, which express themselves abstractly and not in real life between man and man. It follows thus that idealistic philosophy as formulated by Hegel must remove reality in all of its varied states and qualities in order to provide a transparent world absorbed in consciousness.

Feuerbach rejected this point of departure and described the route he himself followed in his personal development. He had set out as a devoted student of Hegel and as a defender of his theory; step by step he moved away from his master's world and arrived at an opposite point of departure. Attesting to this change, Feuerbach himself said that God was his first thought, reason his second, and man his third. What significance does this outline of the stages in the development of his thought have?

These three stages in Feuerbach's personal development express his plan of attack on the walls of the idealistic system as well as his own rounded systematic philosophy. Feuerbach began his thought about God with a philosophical-theological assumption, believed to be self-evident: Thought is bound to true reality, and true reality is the ultimate being, God. Insisting that God is not true ultimate reality, but rather a concept created by the resources of reason, he passed from a theological-metaphysical examination to an examination of the essence of reason; he then turned his investigation from the manifestations of reason to reason itself, which to him was identical with all spiritual pursuits. Methodologically, this transition distinguished the mature Feuerbach: He turned from the creation to the creator, from the branch to the root. He tried to show that God is not an independent reality—conceived as the fundamental principle in every religious view—but dependent upon an even more basic force—reason. Yet, this could not be the end. Feuerbach took the third step: He turned from reason to man. Again the method was the same. Questioning the independent authority of the manifestations, he sought the root that gave life to them. Reason is no longer the ultimate root, for reason itself is but a manifestation of man. The true subject of everything is man.

In the three stages of Feuerbach's development a transition was made from the abstract to the real, from the manifestations of man to the ultimate origin, which was, for him, man in the process of revealing himself. He thus held that philosophy and reason were both dependent on the factual man.

Feuerbach, therefore, suggested a change in the point of departure of contemplative thought. He wished to transfer the domain of contemplation to man, i.e., to transfer theology, the theory of God, to anthropology, the theory of man. In place of abstract reason, he posited man as the full-blooded reality. Man had been a lowly figure in Hegel's system, or, as Feuerbach said in his expressive language, a footnote to the text; now man assumed chief importance as the text itself.

Feuerbach's new approach can be presented from three points of view: (1) He sought to understand concrete man—man in his everyday life. He ceased to be concerned mainly with the analysis of abstract historical and spiritual creations for their own sake. To the extent that he voiced his opinions about the creations—and he did deal with one of them, religion, as we shall see—he did so out of his desire to understand men and not to comprehend the creations themselves. (2) Feuerbach considered man to be essentially a perceiving and sensing being, not an abstractly reasoning being. For the well-known statement of Descartes, "I think, therefore I am," Feuerbach substituted the statement, "I sense, therefore I am." (3) The real perceiving man, within whom all cogitation takes place, cannot be separated from his social reality, according to Feuerbach. Real man is man in the company of man, the man with whom a network of relationships is formed. The "I" and the "Thou" are the true human reality.

Certain positive implications derive from Feuerbach's change in point of departure. His shift from reason to sensation does away with the need for a logical and rational proof of the reality of the world. The very nature of the approach to the world through sensation is that thus the world is perceived directly, giving assurance of its reality. The certainty of reality cannot be questioned, for in sensation men are well situated in a domain that possesses its own certainty, independent of any analysis. As long as men are bound within the world of reason, they are stationed in a world composed of many links, but even when one link is attached to another, the construction itself lacks ultimate solidity. Feuerbach sought to replace such a complicated rational framework with the deep and solid simplicity of sensation. Whatever is perceived by sense experience is not open to doubt. Men are engaged in a realm that does not require any proof whatsoever. The immediate confrontation of the sensation of man with the world is the most basic level of human reality.

One of Feuerbach's most significant moves, then, was from thinking man, who is an aloof entity, to the real man, who is a social creature. In this realm of human association the real subject matter of dialectic, that is, the fusion of opposites into a unity, is found. According to Feuerbach, however, the dialectic is realized in action, not enclosed within a world of abstraction or of shadows, referred to by Hegel as the pure logical forms. In the area of social intercourse, men become involved in a sphere of reality in which the two axes of the dialectical tension, i.e., unity and plurality, are factually realized. Sociality means the fusion of peoples, an interconnection between them, and the creation of relationships between man and his fellow man. From this point of view, sociality is a unity. However, the unity of interrelationships does not do away with the reality of separate individuals involved in these relationships. Sociality exists because of the individuality of the people who interconnect without losing their identity within such a connection. In the domain of society, therefore, the dialectic is realized in actuality either by the unity of a plurality or by unity within a plurality.

Feuerbach analyzed the concept of love as he had that of the social relationship. (Love had occupied Hegel in his early writings, but these were unknown in Feuerbach's time, and Marx too was not familiar with them.) Feuerbach viewed the relationships between the sexes as relationships of love, because love is the bridge between individually different people whose very difference places them in a unifying realm. At the stage of sensation in human activity, love is the clearest expression of social interrelationship. In fact, from this point on, Feuerbach viewed the dialectic as the unity of plurality realized in the concrete world by aid of the concrete relationship of love.

On this basis, Feuerbach rejected the view that the dialectic world appears solely in reason and speculation. He saw the true dialectic actualized instead in the concurrence of experience and reason, as in the coincidence of optics and logic, subjects that Feuerbach had studied, as he said, in a German village and at a German university, respectively. The opposition of optics and logic was an attempt to emphasize the difference between real experience and reason. Feuerbach's theory gave clear preference to the primary position of experience.

From Theology to Anthropology. The most prominent and famous aspect of Feuerbach's theory was his criticism of religion. How did he arrive at this criticism from his theoretical point of departure? Feuerbach set out to determine the essence of religion, which constituted, in his opinion, an introduction to, and the means of determining, the essence of man. What gives religion this distinctive capacity as a key to the understanding of man? Feuerbach pointed out that religion is a phenomenon found only in the realm of man, not in any other. Animals have no religion, and this helps clarify the connection between man and religion. Where does the phenomenon of religion originate—in the essence of man or else in human reality? What enables man to create religion?

Man is a creature capable of seeing and valuing not only himself but also his fellow men, members of his species and his species in general—herein Feuerbach found the origin of religion. The very sociality that he saw as the fundamental principle of the essence of man is also the root of religion. In being aware of his species, man goes beyond the limits of his own self and refers to what lies beyond him as real and given in perception. The relation to his species is a relation to the infinite reservoir of human potentialities rather than to a finite and limited human individual.

This psychological background, or background in consciousness, however, is not yet religion proper. Religion comes into being, Feuerbach thought, when man sees his own essence manifested no longer in himself, or within the limits of his human existence or the existence of his species, but in an ultimate being, a nebulous existence apprehended as absolute perfection.

For Feuerbach, this projective propensity took the form of an appeal, a feeling of the deficiency of the heart. He alluded to the saying of the mystic, Sebastian Frank, that God is the inexpressible languish of the depth of the soul, showing the tension between the feeling of imperfection of human reality and the embodiment of the human essence in a being beyond man. Accordingly, Feuerbach wrote that the emptier the lives of man, the fuller and more concrete is God. The vacuity of the real world and the plenitude of God are one act. Only indigent man has an opulent God. God emerges from man's feeling of exigency.[7] The tension between human reality as such and the human ideal is formed and fortifies itself in religion qua the dichotomy between real man and the ideal man, or God. Religion is nothing but man's awareness of his essence, not an actual manifestation of his real essence with all its deficiencies, but his perfect, infinite, and unlimited essence.[8]

This characteristic of religion reflects the human consciousness of man. By viewing God as an ideal man, Feuerbach held, we can understand man himself. With its history and changes, religion functions as a mirror of man or a floodlight for the comprehension of man, the creator of religion. In the descrip-

[7] Ludwig Feuerbach, "Das Wesen des Christentums," *Ludwig Feuerbach's Sämmtliche Werke,* ed. Wilhelm Bolin and Friedrich Jodl (Stuttgart: F. Frommann, 1903), VI, p. 90.

[8] Feuerbach, p. 17.

tion of the projection of the human essence of man beyond himself, however, the nature of religion has not yet been uncovered. Religion does not consist solely of the inner division of man, in which he splits into the real and the ideal; the attempt is made in religion to bridge the gap between these two realms, which are separated from each other. In religion, man worships himself. He is alienated from himself and attempts to bring under control the being he has extricated from within. The absolute being, the God of man, is the very essence of man himself. The power of the object of man is therefore the power of his own essence.[9] Religion, at least the Christian religion, is the relation of man to himself, or, better, to his own essence; however, the relation to man's own essence is like a relation to another essence.[10]

Feuerbach considered the duality of man, his division between real and ideal, and the actual submission of the real to the ideal to be *the* problem of his age. The time had come to discard religion in order to do away with the transcendent position of man's ideal. The task of man was to humanize and actualize God; in other words, to restore the ideal of man to the limits of man himself. Feuerbach expressed this idea of the actualizing of God or the returning of man to himself metaphorically. He said that the impure baptismal waters must be converted into the pure waters of reality, or that it is worthy to cease being a candidate of the world beyond—a reference to students of theology—and to become a student of this world. The actualization of God is the transformation of theology into anthropology—a transformation that Feuerbach viewed as the core of his system.

This approach provided Feuerbach with a criterion for the determination of the different stages of religion. Before finding it within, man initially locates his essence beyond himself. The essence of man at first looks like a different essence—an object. Religion is the infant essence of humanity. As religion

[9] Feuerbach, p. 6.
[10] Feuerbach, p. 17.

develops historically, what was considered by primitive religion to be objective is now perceived to be subjective; in other words, what was apprehended and prayed to as God now presents itself as something human. In relation to the religion that succeeded it, primitive religion is idolatry: Man always prayed to his own essence.[11] As religion develops, man becomes familiar with the previous levels of religion as the strengthening factors of the human essence. Feuerbach held that now the true character of religion had been revealed, the time had arrived to recognize the idolatrous nature of all religions as such, not only the idolatrous nature of the primitive stages of certain religions. His historical-philosophical idea that the time for the pursuit of human maturity and the elimination of religion had arrived meant that the inclusion of the ideal of man into man himself was the true manifestation of the pursuit of this maturity.

A positive aspect of Feuerbach's theory accompanied this negative aspect, in terms of the criticism of religion. Feuerbach provided a new affirmation to replace the affirmation manifested in religion, saying: I negate the imaginative essence of religion and theology only to affirm the true essence of man. The argument forming the conclusion of his book, *The Essence of Christianity,* implied that religion is folly, nothing, simply an illustration of the nature of man. But religion's foundation is not an illusion, since religion is based on man, and he is a real entity to be studied in anthropology. In reducing theology to anthropology, Feuerbach felt that he lifted anthropology to the level of theology.[12]

Feuerbach did not want to do away with the human content of religion, only with the hypostasis of this content as an entity separated from man. He said that the transformation of theology to anthropology implied a definite action on the part of man. He held that the negation of the world beyond

[11] Feuerbach, p. 16.
[12] Feuerbach, p. 287.

implies the affirmation of *this* world. The elimination of the superior life of heaven implies that life will necessarily be better here on earth. Feuerbach transformed the supreme future from a mere object of faith to an object of duty and independent human activity.[13] He wanted to learn from religion about the essence of man in order to present to man the goal for his own human pursuits. The content of religion is maintained, but it is relegated to the area of man. The object of sensation is beyond man. The object of religion is within him. It is the object of intimacy, even the most intimate, the closest object. God, said St. Augustine, is closer to us, and therefore it is easier to know him than the sensed corporeal things. Feuerbach attempted to preserve the intimate content of religion in order to transform it into the content of human consciousness and thus supplement his merely destructive criticism of religion, the content of which was nonhuman qua divine. Two aspects of religion are thus established in Feuerbach's criticism: *Theoretically,* religion serves as a vantage point for the clarification of the essence of man; *practically,* it serves as a training ground for the freeing of the powers of man.

Feuerbach's position in the development of philosophical and social thought after the death of Hegel was determined in the two problems discussed, being the main problems of the period. In keeping with the members of the leftist wing of the Hegelian school, Feuerbach wanted to eliminate religion. This elimination, however, did not necessarily follow Hegel's theory, in which religion was relegated to a lower stage than philosophy. Feuerbach eliminated religion in dealing with the second problem of the school—the problem of the relationship between concrete reality and reason. He eliminated in the name of reality all systematic formulations on the ground that every system—including religion and speculative philosophy—is bound to be severed both from man and reality. In Feuerbach's theory, the two problems of the Hegelian school

[13] Feuerbach, p. 358.

seem to be linked together. Religion and speculative philosophy are abandoned for the sake of the concrete man and his concrete experience.[14]

PURGATORY

The extent of Marx's relationships to Feuerbach is not a question to which research has found a univocal answer. Johann Plenge, one of the first to examine the philosophical theses of Marx in his *Marx and Hegel*,[15] rejected completely the possibility of such an influence. Yet Engels presented contrary evidence in his book on Feuerbach. There Engels told of the influence that Feuerbach's book, *The Essence of Christianity* had:

> Then came Feuerbach's "Wesen des Christenthums." With one blow it cut the contradiction [between materialism and idealism] . . . it placed materialism on the throne again. Nature exists independently of all philosophies. . . . the higher beings . . . are . . . only fantastic reflections of our individuality. . . . One must himself have experienced the delivering power of this book to get a clear idea of it. . . . We all became . . . followers of Feuerbach.[16]

Moses Hess was perhaps the first to be influenced by Feuerbach and to make his theory the point of departure for a

[14] On the development of the ideas of the generation after Hegel, *see* Sidney Hook, *From Hegel to Marx: Studies in the Intellectual Development of Karl Marx* (New York: Reynal & Hitchcock, 1936); *also* Karl Löwith, *Von Hegel bis Nietzche* (Zurich and New York: Europa, 1941).

On Feuerbach and his method, *see* Friedrich Jodl, *Ludwig Feuerbach* (Stuttgart: F. Frommann, 1904); Simon Rawidowicz, *Ludwig Feuerbach's Philosophie: Ursprung und Schicksal* (Berlin: Reuther & Reichard, 1931); *and* Friedrich Engels, *Ludwig Feuerbach and the Outcome of Classical German Philosophy,* ed. C. P. Dutt (London: M. Lawrence, 1934).

[15] Dr. Johann Plenge, *Marx und Hegel* (Tübingen: H. Laupp'sche Buchhandlung, 1911).

[16] Engels, *Feuerbach and the Outcome of Classical German Philosophy,* p. 53.

theory dealing with questions of society, stressing the projective character of money.

The influence of Feuerbach on Marx should not be exaggerated, however. It can be said generally that Marx assimilated certain elements from Feuerbach's theory into his own system. An examination of these elements will enable us to understand the theses of Marx's system, which he formulated as an argument against Feuerbach.

Marx's "Economic-Philosophic Manuscripts"—written in 1844 and published posthumously in 1932—were recognized for their decisive value in the development of his ideas. There he wrote that his new positive criticism owed its thanks to the discoveries of Feuerbach. It was Feuerbach who effected the positive humanistic and naturalistic criticism, that is to say, a criticism of certain historical and cultural phenomena. Moreover, he attempted to understand these phenomena by means of the natural man. Marx added that Feuerbach's essays were the only ones containing critical analysis. Note the last word, "analysis," which refers to a fact Marx was soon to reveal: Feuerbach's approach still remained within the limits of analysis, and it did not touch directly on questions of practicality. He placed opposite the Hegelian view of philosophy a new positive and true view, sensualism, the positing of what is perceptually indubitable.[17]

In one well-formulated statement involving a play on words, Marx indicated Feuerbach's position in the history of thought. Marx said that there is no way to truth and freedom other than the way of *Feuer-Bach,* that is, "river of fire." Feuerbach is the purgatory of the present.[18] This positive statement of Feuerbach's position contains implicitly an important reservation. Marx did not indicate the systematic conclusions in Feuerbach's theory that had inherent validity. He saw the theory, rather, as a stage of transition, an introductory stage

[17] *MEGA,* I, 3, p. 151; Marx, "Economic and Philosophical Manuscripts," trans. T. B. Bottomore, in Erich Fromm, *Marx's Concept of Man* (New York: Frederick Ungar, 1961), p. 172.

[18] *MEGA,* I, 1, pp. 174–175.

to a riper theory. Perhaps Engels' words above (p. 20) also refer to this liberating significance of Feuerbach's theory. Marx measured the theory from the point of view of the possible conclusions that follow from it and point beyond it; he did not evaluate it in and of itself. This restrained affirmation was also implied in Marx's significant words in the opening of his essays on the criticism of Hegel's *Philosophy of Law*. There Marx said that the critique of religion is the presupposition to all criticism. Even Marx's criticism of society by an analysis of bourgeois economics depended on the criticism of religion, although it went beyond it.

The essential reason why Marx saw in the critique of religion the presupposition of all criticism is that he, as did Feuerbach, viewed religion as the externalization of the ideal essence of man, hypostatized in the heavenly domain beyond man. They both thought that religion is intimately connected with an imperfection prevalent among men, namely, that they fail to realize the full extent of their potentialities. But this analysis of the essence of religion led Marx to the conclusion that the revelation of the essence does not suffice; the condition of man that gave rise to religion must be eliminated. Therefore, Marx, who saw the essence of religion through the eyes of Feuerbach, held to Feuerbach's view in order to criticize the human reality that gave birth to religion in general. From this aspect as well, the critique of religion is the supposition of all criticism, although only a qualified supposition.[19]

Beyond the domain of religion, traces of Feuerbach's theory are to be found in Marx. The methodological aspect, mainly dwelt on here, is also relevant for the aspect of content. The basic point of Feuerbach—a point Marx brought up in his "Manuscripts"—was the attempt to attribute the manifestations of man to man himself. Marx called this method the "method of inversion," conceiving it as a refusal to accept the assumption of the separate existence of various cultural crystallizations and as an attempt to reveal their sources. From this

[19] The exposition of the idea of alienation follows from this; the sources of alienation are analyzed and clarified in Chapter 7 below.

standpoint, Marx regarded his view as radical, in the literal sense of the Latin term *"radix,"* meaning "root." Marx used the method of inversion in all domains, especially in that with which he was mainly concerned, the criticism of society and economy.

In one of his early essays, "On the Jewish Question," Marx had already employed the method of inversion in a positive direction, i.e., in an attempt to attribute the world of man to man. There he said that all emancipation is the restoring of the world of human conditions to man himself.[20] In this context Marx had already expanded the method of inversion to apply to the realms of society and the state, refusing to employ it in the area of religion alone. In thus broadening the use of the method of inversion, Marx used an expression, "conditions," which was to become of pre-eminent importance in the formulation of his theory; "conditions" refers to the social and political framework of man's life. The concept was given an exact reference when it became the subject for the critique of economics.

It is worthwhile to note the employment of the ideas of Feuerbach by the mature Marx. In one section of *Capital,* Marx emphasizes the similarity between man's position in religion and economics. There he stated: "As in religion where man is governed by his brain, so in capitalistic production he is governed by his own hand." [21] Marx's theory of the "fetishist" character of capitalistic economy, in which man is enslaved to the system of goods and commodities that he produces, is actually an expression of his expansion of Feuerbach's method.[22]

[20] Marx, *Der historische Materialismus,* I, p. 255.

[21] Marx, *Das Kapital: Kritik der politischen Ökonomie* (Hamburg: O. Meissner, 1922), I, p. 585; and Marx, *Capital: A Critical Analysis of Capitalist Production,* trans. Samuel Moore and Edward Aveling from 3d German edn. (London: Glaisher, 1912), pp. 634–635. Further reference is made to this work in Chapter 7 below.

[22] Rawidowicz, *Feuerbach's Philosophie,* pp. 411 ff.; Löwith, *Von Hegel bis Nietzsche,* p. 130; *see also* Herbert Marcuse, *Reason and Revolution: Hegel and the Rise of Social Theory* (London and New York: Oxford University Press, 1941).

The common ground between Marx and Feuerbach occurs, then, in their mutual aim to "realize" God and to eliminate the split between the ideal and the real within human existence. However, Marx sought to find this division in part beyond the sphere of religion. Marx was akin to Feuerbach in that Marx employed the method of inversion, which permanently based philosophizing on man himself. He introduced a different theory from that of Feuerbach, however. This becomes clear in his "Theses on Feuerbach."

CHAPTER 2

Karl Marx: Theses on Feuerbach[1]

1

The main shortcoming of all materialism up to now (including that of Feuerbach) is that the object, the reality, sensibility, is conceived only in the form of the *object* or of the *perception* [*Anschauung*], but not as sensuous human activity, *practice* [*Praxis*], not subjectively. Hence, the *active* side was developed abstractly in opposition to materialism by idealism, which naturally does not know the real, sensuous activity as such. Feuerbach urged the real distinction between sensuous activity and thought objects; but he does not conceive of human activity itself as an *objective* [*gegenständlich*] activity. Hence, he deals in *Essence of Christianity* only with the theoretical attitude, as genuinely human, while practice is conceived and determined only in its dirty-Jewish form of appearance. He therefore does not apprehend the significance of the "revolutionary," practical-critical activity.

2

The question whether objective truth is to be assigned to human thinking is not a question of theory, but a practical question. In practice, man is bound to prove the truth, that is,

[1] I have attempted to make a faithful translation from the German text; it is often a literal translation.

the reality and force, the this-worldliness of his thinking. The dispute over the reality or nonreality of his thinking isolated from practice is a pure *scholastic* question.

3

The materialistic teaching on the changing of the circumstances and education forgets that the circumstances are changed by men, and it is necessary that the educator himself be educated. This teaching, therefore, is bound to split society into two parts, of which one is superior to the other.[2]

The concurrence of changing of the circumstances and of the human activity, or self-changing, can be conceived as *revolutionary practice.*

4

Feuerbach starts out from the fact of religious self-alienation, of duplication of the world into a religious and into a worldly one. His work consists in resolving the religious world into its worldly substratum. But that the worldly substratum sets itself apart from itself and fixes itself in an independent (nebulous) realm, can be explained only by the self-discord and self-contradiction [*Selbstzerrissenheit und Sichselbstwidersprechen*] of this worldly substratum. Therefore, the latter, in itself, as well as in its contradiction, must be understood and practically revolutionized. Hence, for example, once the earthly family is disclosed as the secret of the holy family, the former must now be annihilated both theoretically and practically.

5

Feuerbach, not satisfied with *abstract thinking,* advocates perception; but he does not conceive sensibility as *practical* human-sensuous activity.

[2] This follows the text given in *MEGA,* I, 5: "*von denen der eine über ihr erhaben ist.*" Other editions read *ihn* for *ihr.*

6

Feuerbach resolves the religious essence into the *human* essence. But the human essence is not an abstract, inherent in the single individual. In its reality it is the ensemble of the social conditions.

Feuerbach does not go into the criticism of this real essence, and is, therefore, compelled (1) to abstract from the historical course of events, to fix a religious mental disposition, and to presume an abstract–*isolated*–human individual; (2) the essence can therefore be conceived only as "species," as inward, mute generality, binding the many individuals *naturally*.

7

Feuerbach does not see, therefore, that "the religious mental disposition" itself is a social product and that the abstract individuum, whom he analyzes, belongs to a particular form of society.

8

All social life is essentially *practical*. All mysteries that induce theory to mysticism find their rational solution in human practice and in the conception of this practice.

9

The highest that perception-materialism [*der anschauende Materialismus*] reaches, that is, the materialism that does not conceive of sensibility as practical activity, is the perception of the single individuals in the civil society.[3]

[3] *"Bürgerliche Gesellschaft,"* sometimes translated as "bourgeois society." The accepted terminology of English translations of Hegel is adopted here.

CHAPTER 3

Theses on Materialism

FIRST THESIS: OLD AND NEW MATERIALISM

The main shortcoming of all materialism up to now (including that of Feuerbach) is that the object, the reality, sensibility, is conceived only in the form of the *object* or of the *perception,* but not as sensuous human activity, *practice,* not subjectively. Hence, the *active* side was developed abstractly in opposition to materialism by idealism, which naturally does not know the real, sensuous activity as such. Feuerbach urged the real distinction between sensuous activity and thought objects; but he does not conceive of human activity itself as an *objective* activity. Hence, he deals in *Essence of Christianity* only with the theoretical attitude, as genuinely human, while practice is conceived and determined only in its dirty-Jewish form of appearance. He therefore does not apprehend the significance of the "revolutionary," practical-critical activity.

"All materialism up to now." This description refers primarily to French materialism of the second half of the eighteenth century, a philosophical movement the main representatives of which were Julien Offroy de la Mettrie, Claude Adrien Helvétius, and Paul Henri Dietrich d'Holbach. Limiting the discussion of materialism to the context of the first thesis alone, such materialists sought to account for the universal order of the world. The world is basically material, they held. In the universal laws and in the all-embracing material reality, no particular is to be found for man. Man is a machine—the title

of La Mettrie's book—and he can be conceived of as a large clock, working in accordance with mechanistic law.[1]

"The main shortcoming" is that this materialism relates to reality only theoretically. The principal instrument of man's relation to the universe is sense observation, not pure reason and abstract thinking. But the changing of the instrument does not suffice to change the theoretical aim of materialism "up to now." As a further consequence of the theoretical objective, under this materialism the world and man are apprehended simply as objects that knowledge, now taken as nonrational, sensuous observation, seeks to understand. Hence, this materialism contains a passive trend. It sees man as absorbing impressions of given reality and nothing more. The theory implies, as Holbach said, that will is necessarily determined by the good or bad nature of the object or by the drive toward it. Human action follows from the impulse originating in this drive. Man is determined by given factors, this doctrine maintains, and hence is fundamentally receptive and passive.

"Including that of Feuerbach." Marx included the view of Feuerbach in the trend of materialism "up to now," the form of materialism in which the French movement was dominant. Although the practical aspect was not omitted in Feuerbach's theory, Marx still interpreted Feuerbach's conception as bound to the trend of theoretical materialism, the very materialism that sought to understand reality through sense observation.

[1] In a previous essay, "The Holy Family" (*"Die Heilige Familie"*), 1843, Marx stressed the practical conclusions that followed from the French materialistic school, in terms of natural equality of human intellectual capacities, the unity between the progress of reason and the progress of industry, the natural goodness of man, and the omnipotence of education (*MEGA,* I, 3, pp. 300–301). In the present thesis a change seems to emerge in Marx's evaluation of French materialism; the third thesis testifies to this as well. Marx's interest in materialism in the philosophical sense had been already expressed in his doctoral dissertation, entitled "Differenz der Demokritischen und Epikureischen Naturphilosophie, nebst einem Anhang," submitted at Jena in 1841.

As early as 1843, in a letter to Arnold Ruge, Marx had written that what was missing in Feuerbach's aphorisms was sufficient emphasis on the political aspect. This remark can be understood in the light of the argument in the first thesis: the absence of emphasis on the political aspect amounts to the failure to emphasize human practice as the foundation of the new view on the essence of man. Hence, Feuerbach "wants sensuous objects"; he prefers *objects* and does not seek to understand the force that creates the objects, which is itself practice grounded in the subject, the active man.

This argument against Feuerbach was of pre-eminent importance in the criticism that Marx employed against the young, left-wing Hegelian school. Because the members of the left wing still held fast to the sphere of theory and had not as yet passed to the sphere of practical action, Marx argued, they deemed it sufficient to change their view of the world in order to change the world itself. It seemed to the members of the school that the change, or the crisis, needed only to be reflected through a change in the consciousness of man. A theoretical approach to the world implies the restriction of change to the theoretical domain. From this standpoint, no actual change takes place in reality itself. This characteristic of the attitude of the Hegelian school makes the allegedly effected change an imaginary one, because it remains an abstract change only. Not only does reality remain unchanged, but by means of a new elucidation of reality, it is even acknowledged as such. This new elucidation, *post factum,* and perhaps also from the outset, is no more than an attempt at "conciliation" with given reality. It is certainly not an attempt to substitute it for another reality.[2]

The absence of the practical aspect that characterized Feuerbach's view of materialism implies an absence of connection between this materialism and history or else this materialism

[2] *MEGA,* I, 3, p. 9; Karl Marx and Friedrich Engels, *The German Ideology,* trans. and ed., with introductions, by R. Pascal (New York: International Publishers, 1947), p. 5.

lacks a view of history. In this context, Marx said of Feuerbach: Insofar as Feuerbach is a materialist, he does not mention history, and insofar as he voices his opinion about history, he is no longer a materialist. Materialism and history are completely separate for him.[3]

What can be concluded? Materialism "up to now," including Feuerbach's view as materialism, is based on nature, and man himself is perceived as nature. The relation to nature is a theoretical one, and from the point of view of a theoretical relationship, man and nature are viewed as objects.

"Practice is conceived and determined only in its dirty-Jewish form of appearance." To be sure, Feuerbach knew of the practical side of man; however, he saw it as an inferior side, as indicated in the chapter on Judaism in his book *The Essence of Christianity*. There Feuerbach interpreted the Jewish conception of God and exposed the idea of creation of the world *ex nihilo* as the fundamental idea of Judaism. Judaism views the world as the fruit of the will of God, and this will in turn is the ruling power in the world. According to Feuerbach, this idea of predominance of will was to be conceived as the projection of man himself. Man who understands will as the ultimate power, understands the world as the product of will. Therefore, man, whose relation to the world is one of will, seeks to use this world, to enjoy it, and to derive benefit from it. Will and utility are interconnected; they are two aspects of the same thing.

Feuerbach held, therefore, that utility is the ultimate principle of Judaism, and that the theory of creation that sees creation as a product of will is nothing but a theoretical formulation of the egoism of the Jew. However, Feuerbach thought Christianity, the highest stage in the development of religions, went beyond the practical-egoistical-utilitarian view of Judaism. In Christianity the center of the theory is no longer found in the relation of man to the world but in the relation of man to himself, and therefore the God of Christianity is not en-

[3] *MEGA,* I, 3, p. 34; Pascal, pp. 37–38.

tirely a ruling God. He is a God possessing inner life that reflects the rich inner life of man. In comparison to the egoistic view of Juadism, Christianity appears as a subjectivistic religion. This subjectivity, however, is but a corollary of the repression of the real activity of man. According to Feuerbach, as Marx interpreted him, the active relation to the world was not of primary human importance, but lay on a lower level of the development of man. Of primary importance was the theoretical relation.[4]

This view of Judaism is found in the second part of Marx's essay "On the Jewish Question," where his well-known evaluation of Judaism appears. Marx's argument there is merely a summary of the position of Feuerbach; yet, it must be observed that the word "dirty" is not found in Feuerbach.[5]

"The active *side was developed . . . in opposition to materialism by idealism."* The active side of knowing is revealed according to Marx in idealism, and it is possible to explain this point in two ways. (1) Knowing is not apprehended by the idealist as a passive receiving of the world or a passive recording of impressions. The idealistic conception of mind implies its constructive character. Idealists, in contradistinction to materialists, who apprehend knowing as do the epistemological realists, do not know fixed and ordered real substances that must be photographed, so to speak, in thought. Idealists view things as constructed by the mind itself; a thing is nothing but a group of characteristics defined by the mind. Objects are nothing but objectifications. (2) The fundamental basis of

[4] Ludwig Feuerbach, "Das Wesen des Christentums," *Ludwig Feuerbach's Sämmtliche Werke,* ed. Wilhelm Bolin and Friedrich Jodl (Stuttgart: F. Frommann, 1903), VI, Ch. 2.

[5] Marx's relation to Feuerbach on this matter is discussed in Simon Rawidowicz, *Ludwig Feuerbach's Philosophie: Ursprung und Schicksal* (Berlin: Reuther & Reichard, 1931); *see also* Nathan Rotenstreich, "For and Against Emancipation: The Bruno Bauer Controversy," *Year Book* LIV, publication of the Leo Baeck Institute of Jews from Germany (London: East and West Library, 1959), esp. pp. 3 ff., 23 ff.

idealism, and most explicitly the idealism of Hegel, is mind, or Spirit. Reality is apprehended by idealists as the manifestation of the mind, or Spirit, and the development of reality is the development of Spirit. Spirit is defined as spontaneous, as a free self-determination.[6] The unique nature of Spirit is that it is not dependent upon motivating forces outside it. It is the mover, and it is the moved. Idealism, then, is related to Marx's theory of knowledge—that is, the idealism of Kant and Hegel—and to the hypothesis about the character of mind, or Spirit, and knowing, manifested in reality. Marx indicates this dynamic aspect elsewhere, stating that the important point in Hegel's *The Phenomenology of the Spirit* is that he apprehends the self-creation of man as a process.[7] Here, the two words "self-creation" and "process" can be emphasized, the former pointing to Spirit as the final origin or its own origin, and the latter pointing to the independent creation as *process,* manifesting the dynamic and active character of idealism.

"Abstractly . . . , which naturally does not know the real, sensuous activity as such." Yet Marx argued that idealism exposes activity as activity of Spirit and not of the real man, as spiritual activity and not real, sensuous activity. The idealism of Hegel assumes the World-Spirit, not real man, as the final subject for history. Man is the implement in the hands of this Spirit, and this Spirit is not a manifestation of man. Herein Marx criticized the trend of idealism from the position of Feuerbach's basic assumptions. Whereas idealism places activity in the abstract area of mind and knowing, Marx stressed practice in the area of man himself. Therefore Marx said in his "Paris Manuscripts"—which are of decisive significance for the understanding of the formulation of his theory—that Hegel found only an abstract expression, speculative and logical, for

[6] Georg Hegel, *Encyklopädie der philosophischen Wissenschaften: Sämtliche Werke* (Leipzig: F. Meiner, 1932–1934), V, par. 383.

[7] *MEGA,* I, 3, p. 156; Marx, "Economic and Philosophical Manuscripts," trans. T. B. Bottomore, in Erich Fromm, *Marx's Concept of Man* (New York: Frederick Ungar, 1961), p. 176.

the movement of history, and that his theory was not based on the actual history of man as the proper subject of history. Furthermore, Marx held, the synthesis reached by Hegelian idealism was a synthesis in the realm of consciousness, or a synthesis in the realm of pure thought only.[8]

These observations demonstrate how Marx viewed the historical-systematic position of his own theory. Marx rejected materialism "up to now," because it lacked a practical side. He rejected idealism because the active side in it appeared only from the point of view of abstract Spirit. He urged a synthesis that would integrate sensuousness as projected by materialism and activity as projected by idealism. The actual practice of the actual man, therefore, became central to his system. Practice is the practice of a natural creature—as distinguished from and opposed to an abstract creature—who creates actual objects. Marx himself established this synthetic position. His theory was given two names: *naturalism,* which brought into prominence the natural side, or the domain of the natural-real-sensuous in which his theory was grounded; and *humanism,* which brought into prominence not nature external to man and the world of things subsuming man but man himself. Naturalism and humanism were, according to Marx, to be distinguished from both materialism and idealism, although they continued to be the unifying factors of these two contending philosophical streams.[9]

The actual expression of this synthesis was the new view, which in its later development was called *historical materialism.* This view was materialistic, because it claimed to apprehend the sensuous phase of human reality, the same phase that traditional materialism explicated in the relation of man to the exterior world or to nature. But it was a *historical* materialism because it hinged on the sensuous axis; it did not hinge on the basis of the relation of man to the external world, but on the basis of the relationship of man to himself. The reality by which man relates to himself is a historical reality.

[8] *MEGA,* I, 3, p. 155; Bottomore, p. 176.
[9] *MEGA,* I, 3, p. 160; Bottomore, p. 182.

Hence, Marx, in his work, "The German Ideology," for which the "Theses on Feuerbach" served as a preparatory exercise, called his theory practical materialism. He added that this materialism was the same as communism.[10] The main principle of this materialism lay in the discovery that the historical life of man was practical by its very nature.

Marx's chain of ideas is evinced when its dependence upon the fundamental assumption of the active character of man is seen. The active character of man reaches its complete manifestation in history. The connection between the actual practice of man and his historical life is apprehended when it is viewed from the perspective of active man; in other words, it is observed from the standpoint of active or historical materialism.

"Sensuous human activity, practice." This real activity, the basis of the new theory, is called *Praxis*. What is the core of this real practice? What is the distinguishing characteristic of man? In "German Ideology," Marx stated in words directed undoubtedly against Feuerbach:

> Men can be distinguished from animals by consciousness, by religion, or anything else you like. They themselves begin to distinguish themselves from animals as soon as they begin to *produce* their means of subsistence, a step which is conditioned by their physical organization. By producing their means of subsistence men are indirectly producing their actual material life.[11]

Thus the actual activity of human beings is production, in the economic sense of the term, and production even becomes the identifying characteristic of man. This characteristic is no longer to be found in the realm of consciousness; consciousness itself is not man's distinctive feature. Practice viewed as production, the very root of the historical life of man, is also the identifying feature of man.

Production has two main aspects: It creates both the wants

[10] *MEGA,* I, 5, p. 32; Pascal, p. 37.
[11] *MEGA,* I, 5, p. 10; Pascal, p. 6.

and the means for the provision of goods. The goods are not absolute and unchangeable; they change through production itself. Marx called this system of wants and the provision of goods "the production of material life." It is a historical process, for it is connected to the root of historical life, the real practice of man. The involvement of the process of production in historical life and the dynamics implied in this system draw the line separating Marx's theory from the traditional theory of economics, which he had studied but against which he argued fundamentally. Production is the first historical realization of practice, the identifying characteristic of man. The first historical act is, therefore, the creation of the means for providing goods, the production of material life itself, the fundamental condition of all history. It is clear on this matter that the theory by and large identified with historical materialism stresses the conditioning position of economics in the historical process. The connection between economics as a dynamic process and practice explains again the position of economics in Marx's theory. Economics from the point of view of production is the first historical practice, or the first historical act, in accordance with the way Marx formulated the idea as described above.

At this point the problematic nature of the theory must be considered. Is it a historical act *first,* in the order of time alone, or is its nature as a first act preserved in the historical process in general, the first act, temporally speaking, being always the *conditioning* act from the point of view of content? Marx has actually presented us with a double formulation, which seeks to couple the idea in its two aspects: Production is the first historical act in the order of time, and it is a fundamental condition of all history, apparently, from the point of view of content.

"He does not apprehend the significance of the 'revolutionary,' practical-critical activity." The preceding analysis does not exhaust the full content of the concept "practice," as presented in Marx's writings. Marx argued against Feuerbach,

who saw action as a lower level of human life. Action, according to Feuerbach, is connected with the acquisition of pleasure, or with utility; it is egoistic-utilitarian action. A somewhat pointed question arises: Is such an acquisition an action at all? Marx apparently thought that it was not an action, that it did not create objects; it derived pleasure from given objects, insofar as it derived benefit from them. The action that Marx set foremost in his theory was not an action of use and exploitation of goods or objects of the surrounding world; it was rather a creative action, a spontaneous action, even though it was limited to the area of the senses.

Here the roots of the "revolutionary" aspect of practice can be seen in creating reality and changing it. The revolutionary aspect of action is explained further by a clarification of the word "criticism," which Marx used in the same context. Revolutionary action is a critical activity, or the critical activity is revolutionary.

What is the meaning of criticism? Marx himself answered that "Criticism is the measuring of a particular existence according to essence, and a particular reality according to an idea." [12] It is the act of comparison between given reality and the idea of this reality; it is the test whether a given reality corresponds to the idea or realizes it. For example, criticism is the test of given human reality according to the criterion of essential human freedom. This was a step taken by Marx with deep and bitter sarcasm, a step that he called "impudence," that is, the desire to make man into man. In the event that criticism finds that in reality man is not free but is enslaved to himself and to the works of his hands, it is a criticism the meaning of which lies in the evaluation of this specific reality according to the idea of freedom.

This notion of criticism was undoubtedly related to Hegel's theory of the essence of truth. Truth, said Hegel, philosophically speaking, is the "agreement of a thought content with itself," that is, the correspondence of a concept to its reality. By a true friend, according to Hegel, "we mean a friend whose

[12] *MEGA,* I, 1, p. 64.

manner of conduct accords with the notion of friendship. . . . Untrue in this sense means the same as bad, or self-discordant. In this sense a bad state is an untrue state." [13]

Marx's view on criticism can be formulated as follows: criticism examines whether truth actually exists; it examines whether the content corresponds to itself, or, in other words, whether the concept and reality are congruent. The Hegelian assumption made by Marx was that the idea and the reality are fundamentally not separate, and that when they do become separate it is necessary to change the reality by a "revolutionary action," an action capable of creating a new reality. The critical activity is by its own nature a revolutionary activity. It does not begin with the assumption that reality is independent, but with the opposite assumption that reality is the realization of an idea. Marx did not recognize the irreconcilable dualism between reality and the idea; had he done so, there would have been no place for his theory of the revolutionary nature of criticism. However, because the idea and reality are inherently bound in one and the same domain, and because the historical reality of bourgois society divides the two spheres, once again a need exists for the critique of reality separated from the idea in order to actualize the idea in reality by means of a revolutionary act. Revolutionary action has two aspects: The theoretical side of revolutionary action confronts the idea with the reality, and the practical side actualizes the idea within a specific reality for the purpose of creating a new reality. (This is the root of the critique of self-alienation, by which reality is separated from the idea. It is discussed below in Chapter 7.)

It is clear, then, that practice, as real and sensuous activity according to Marx, has two basic functions: It gives rise to historical life in that it produces the actual dynamics of that life, but it also determines the direction of that life, that is, the realization of the idea within historical reality. Now we

[13] Hegel, *Encyklopädie,* par. 24, Zusatz 2; *and* Hegel, "The Logic of Hegel," *Encyclopaedia,* trans. William Wallace (Oxford: Oxford University Press, 1892), p. 52.

can deal with the core of Marx's theory, in which the economic process maintains a decisive position, not only in the determination of history, but also in the building of the new human reality that is, the socialist reality. Production and the process of production are the beginnings of history. They may direct it by revolution, that is, they may actualize the idea within a given reality. Herein the dialectic function of production in Marx's system is revealed, a function that, according to Marx, is merely the expression of the dialectic character of practice. Practice is what creates given human reality and by the same token extricates human reality from the given situation. Practice produces the present situation and overturns it by revolution. Production consists, therefore, of two aspects. Moreover, criticism is not merely theoretical. A theoretical critique would leave the domain of reality as it stands, although placing it on a lower level than the idea and its content, as did many dualistic trends in the history of philosophy. The critique is essentially practical. It is the critique of practice, the critique of the attempt to bridge the gap between the two spheres, and finally, it is not a critique of the stabilization of the spheres in terms of their intrinsic meanings alone. Hence, Marx emphasized that it is practice to which reference is being made, practice as an actual sensuous act. Here criticism is not being implemented by someone on the side who observes the idea and the reality as separate and who evaluates the specific reality in terms of the criterion of the idea. Here—and this is the most important aspect—reality evaluates itself in terms of the idea, and this evaluation of reality is actual, i.e., it is practice.

Returning to the central position of production in Marx's theory, production is the distinctive feature of man. Through production man distinguishes himself from animals. But since production is the defining characteristic of man, it must also actualize this characteristic, the idea of reason. Production brings about history causally; it is also teleologically the actualization of the idea. The dialectic of practice is the dialectic of production and also the dialectic of causal and teleological attitudes respectively. The title of Herbert Marcuse's book, *Reason and Revolution*,[14] may point to this issue. Practice is revolution actualizing the idea of reason. The idea necessitates revolution, because without it, it is not actualized. Revoluion is in need of the idea of reason, because without it revolution does not have content to actualize. From this standpoint, in Marx's system of thought a central task was designated for the concept practice, the arch-concept. This position clarifies the significance of the second thesis as well.

EXCURSUS: REASON, SPIRIT, AND PRACTICE

As shown above, the concept of practice (*Praxis*) was central to Marx's philosophical view. For Marx, the concept of practice as revolution was the expression of the principal force of the historical process and the primary force that brings about future historical change. Though this concept was central for Marx, he himself did not systematically clarify it extensively, so that the significance and function it held in his system could be understood. Marx's ideas on this subject are elucidated here by comparing the concept of practice with other philosophical concepts that arose during the same period and undoubtedly influenced the formation of the central concept of his system. In particular, Marx's concept of practice will be clarified by a comparison with Hegel's concept of Spirit.

Hegel's concept of Spirit, to state its essential nature, was the active identity between consciousness and reality. This identity was in general a matter of reason, for Hegel defined the essence of reason as the certainty of consciousness, which is itself reality. What Hegel called Spirit proper was the development of this identity in reason, the *actualization* of this identity in reality, in such institutions as law and state, and such creations as art, religion, and philosophy. Spirit is the activity of reason actualizing itself within reality and creating it. It is the very spheres of reality, such as state, law, art, and

[14] Herbert Marcuse, *Reason and Revolution* (London, New York, and Toronto: Oxford University Press, 1941).

religion. This is the concerte reality, wherein our real experience lies and our real life takes place. Exemplifying the relationship between reason and Spirit in paragraph 387 of the *Encyklopädie,* Hegel said, "Spirit is related to reason as body is to weight and will to freedom." Spirit, as the active manifestation of reason, is likened to body, which is the active manifestation of weight, and to will, which is the active manifestation of freedom. The body is concealed within weight, in the way that will is the concealed essence of freedom. However, what is concealed and exists in them, as given, and in potentiality, is developed and exists in reality in active manifestations of body and will.

Spirit as the revelation of reason, however, makes this identity with reason active, existent, influential, and hence, expressed in the real process of events. What Hegel stated in this section of the *Encyklopädie* can be expressed somewhat differently: spirit makes the identity between consciousness and reason an identity *acknowledged* by consciousness. Instead of the simple and given identity accompanying awareness and knowledge through Spirit, this identity reaches a point where consciousness knows its true nature insofar as it knows that reality is identical with it. Again, in such Hegelian spheres as state, law, art, religion, and philosophy, consciousness reaches the knowledge of what is concealed within it; consciousness reaches a point of satiety and seeks to understand that it is identical with reality. If it were not for the manifestations of institutions and creativity, consciousness would not be able to understand what is concealed within it. Because of these manifestations consciousness is able to form reality, and by doing this it reaches the supreme level of knowledge, self-knowledge. Thus Hegel could say in paragraph 383 of the *Encyklopädie* that Spirit is identical with self-revelation.

Another aspect of the essence of Spirit calls for further elucidation, even though it has been hinted at above. Spirit is the process of reason that forms and builds the institutions of reality. Spirit is also the activity of contemplation, reflexive as Hegel said, for Spirit is the institutions of reality and their cognition. To put it differently: On the one hand, Spirit is a historical process, and, on the other, the knowledge of this process; by being knowledge, Spirit actualizes itself in the great realms of creation.

In summary, Spirit, according to Hegel, is the dynamic aspect of reason. Hence, Spirit creates history and its real manifestations. However, Spirit also knows the history it has created, via cognition. Spirit is not only identical with history, but brings to light creations contained in the area that Hegel termed "absolute," that is, art, religion, and philosophy. Spirit, according to Hegel, appears as the beginning of the historical process from the standpoint of its creative power, as a process in itself, and as the end of the process from the point of view of its knowledge.[15]

It is suggested that Marx's concept of practice is parallel to Hegel's concept of Spirit and was developed to replace it; and that the relation between practice and theory according to Marx is parallel to the relationship between Spirit and reason according to Hegel. If these suggestions are correct, it must be shown that Marx's concept *practice* replaces Hegel's concept *Spirit,* and not the concept of reason.

In the first thesis, Marx spoke about "sensuous human activity, *practice,* . . . real . . . activity[,] . . . practical-critical activity." In this thesis, Marx substituted practice and activity for observation, in which objects and the world are observed passively and impressions are received from the world, without operating in it. In place of observation and sense impressions, Marx posited the creative attitude that intervenes in the course of events or in the course of history. This attitude or position is identified with that of practice. Since man, according to Marx, is in control of practice, he is a historical creature.

However, practice not only brings about history and maintains it up to the present; practice, as stressed before, is also the force that makes history forge ahead to its new level. It

[15] On Hegel's theory, *see* Nathan Rotenstreich, "Hegel's Concept of Mind," *Revue Internationale de Philosophie,* Vol. XVI, No. 19 (1952), pp. 27–34.

is the force that carries man, the subject of practice, and humanity, in which the practice of man is immersed, from historical reality "up to now"—the reality of necessity and coercion—to a new historical reality, the reality of freedom. Practice modifies the process, changes it, and in so doing ends it.

From this standpoint Marx's concept of practice can be seen to be parallel to Hegel's concept of Spirit. Just as Spirit created process, is aware of it as a fact, and hence transcends it; so practice created process and is also the force that surmounts the process. Yet the difference between Hegel and Marx is also quite clear. The surmounting of the process in Hegel's system is a victory through conception or cognition. It is brought about through great works of art, religion, and philosophy. Yet a victory over process is not, according to Marx, a surmounting of the process of history. It is an overcoming of process up to the present. Marx does not regard this process of history up to the present as the true and adequate sense of the concept of history, because it does not express and evince practice in its essence, that is, it does not actualize man's freedom. The man of practice up to the present is not a free man. If history does not show man to be free, that is evidence that practice is not expressed adequately therein. With the change of one formula of Marx it can be said that practice always exists, not, however, in a form that always is adequate to it. The surmounting of process does not take us outside process, but brings us, according to Marx, to a new stage, to a new initiation of process. Therefore, it may be possible to understand what Marx meant when he spoke about practice in general and about revolutionary practice in particular. Even though his use of terms was not consistent, it can be said, perhaps, that practice in general created the historical process and that revolutionary practice in particular brings about the decisive shift in the position of man so that he becomes the ruler of the circumstances of his life.

Stated in another way, practice is parallel to the concept of Spirit in that practice, like Spirit, is activity. Practice is also parallel to Spirit in that it creates reality and a new dimension of the future of man. For Hegel the new dimension was the dimension of creation and reflection, and it was therefore concerned with art, religion, and philosophy; whereas for Marx the new dimension was concerned with historical reality, it was a new stage in human reality. The surpassing of process took place perpendicularly for Hegel and, therefore, through a *reflection* upon process; whereas the surpassing of process for Marx was on a horizontal line and it was, therefore, a new historical *reality*. It is obvious that the conversion from the perpendicular to the horizontal was what brought about the renowned watchword of "the planting of Hegel on his feet," because reflection, which was for Hegel the surmounting of process, became a part of process and immersed in it. In its stead came the process in its new stage.

It must be emphasized, however, that practice does not come in place of *reason;* it comes in place of Spirit. Practice presupposes the concept of reason, in that the consciousness of the identity between consciousness and reality precedes practice, the creator of the process, which brings forth this identity and materializes it in reality. Practice has a guide in this very identification: Identity is the framework that delimits it and the direction that guides it. The historical process for Marx was the rational process, but reason did not always exist rationally. The objective of practice is to create a correspondence between reason and existence. One cannot speak about a full identity between theory and practice. Inasmuch as the idea of identity between consciousness and reality is theoretical, and it must be theoretical because it is an idea, it precedes the realization of the identity within the historical process. Identity between theory and practice is more than mere theory without practice; however, identity does not replace theory. Metaphorically it can be said that in the beginning there was theory, and its position cannot be expropriated.

If this is the case, and the discussion of the position of practice as the force parallel to Spirit has led to this conclusion, then a question is raised about historical materialism itself. If theory exists without actualization in the identity between theory and practice, the position that theory is entirely determined by the historical process cannot be maintained. The force of theory is independent, and as such it requires the acknowledgment of historical reflection. The basic argument of historical materialism, in terms of which all manifestations of human creativity are historical, is founded on the absence of a clear view of the difference between reason and Spirit, a distinction which Hegel made. History, which is brought about by practice for Marx, replaces history brought about by Spirit according to Hegel, but it does not come in place of reason. The complete historicity of consciousness and of reason are not possible, and hence a perfect balance of the perpendicular is not possible. The analysis of the concept "practice" leads to a conclusion directed against the extravagance of historical materialism. The extent to which the concept of practice is parallel to the concept of Spirit as formulated by Hegel is clear also on examination of the third thesis of Marx on Feuerbach, as will be seen below.

Spirit, then, connotes the manifestations of reason, as well as the consciousness that reality is rational. The identification between the real activity of reason and practice in Marx's sense; or the identification between practice, the activity of reason itself, and what the activity brings about—we shall call this last aspect practice, too—is one of the factors indicating practice for Marx. This triple identification is again similar to the identification within Spirit, in the domain of history, and Spirit and concept in the theoretical field. This last identification undoubtedly has its roots in the doctrine of Hegel. The difference is not in the general character of the analysis, but in the area in which concepts are raised or in which the three are presented in the case before us: in the realm of consciousness in Hegel and the realm of historical process in Marx. But here as well, the trilogy is not of practice and activity; practice substitutes for the mind knowing and the known. The historical trilogy is a means of actualizing the theoretical but does not make the theoretical superfluous.

The question about the process or dynamics of reason was not peripheral in the philosophy of the nineteenth century. The thoughts of Marx were rooted in a tradition that considered the question, and his answer was related to other answers that had been offered. Comparison of an idea of Johann Fichte with the ideas of Hegel and Marx reveals this relationship.

In order to point out the fundamental dynamics of reason, Fichte created a philosophical term that combined two words. This was the concept of *deed-act,* or in German, *Tathandlung.* With the use of this term, Fichte chose to show first, that reason is a free creation that does not presuppose any kind of external element. It creates itself; it is pure activity. Fichte expressed this by saying that the "I" posits itself. Second, however, the activity of which Fichte spoke is an activity of reason in relation to itself; hence, it is a reflexive action, not directed beyond itself. Therefore, the activity for Fichte, the *deed-act,* is the activity of reason within its own limits, not an activity that removes reason from its inherent nature to reality by making it identical with reality.

Here Hegel's thought started, and Marx followed it. Reason for Hegel was in its very essence content-bearing, that is, it is identity. Reason actually comes to know this identity, not only as an inner concealed law but as a law that is rendered real and known by the self-same reason as identity. The inner content of reason brings reason to direct itself toward reality and motivates it to identify with it, whether through institutions or through knowing. Once reason takes on inner content, the movement is no longer directionless; it is a movement that serves identity; it realizes and reveals it.

Marx and Hegel differed in only one aspect. Hegel thought that reason itself was active force, and hence, reason becomes Spirit; whereas Marx thought that reason is used for the purpose of activity of the power of real man, or what he called practice. Practice serves reason by creating the historical process that in turn serves reason and is capable of materializing it within reality. Marx thought that since reason realizes itself within reality, the instrument that renders it real has to be like reality and cannot be an instrument of reason itself. This instrument is "real activity," sensuous as such, as was stated in the first thesis on Feuerbach. Actually, the difference between Marx and Hegel was that Hegel believed that reason is autarchic, possessing instruments capable of materializing itself, whereas Marx believed that reason is dependent upon real man for materialization.[16] Therefore, a distinction enters into Marx's system, which is its central feature, for this system inherently knows man's place within existence as an instrument for actualizing reason. However, man is not without the anchor or compass of reason: practice does not replace reason, a common misunderstanding, but comes on its behalf; practice directs reason and elevates its real activity to the level of the creation of history.

The principal importance of this idea is, therefore, that Marx indirectly proposed a theory of man, but did not develop it properly, mainly because of the raging polemic of his pronouncements, and because he did not present it in a form suitable to its content. Man is not *homo faber,* or, at any rate, he is not merely this. He is *homo sapiens,* and being *homo faber* serves his being *homo sapiens.* Marx is inclined to present his ideas under the assumption that man is *homo faber* alone and does not elucidate the point that his being *homo faber* presupposes his being *homo sapiens.* Marx shows that activity serves reason and fails to show that it is inherent in it.

SECOND THESIS: THEORY AND PRACTICE

> The question whether objective truth is to be assigned to human thinking is not a question of theory, but a

[16] This is the central point of Marx's criticism of Hegel. Marx argues that Hegel made the subject into a predicate, that is to say, Hegel turned reason into the subject and the real-concrete man into a predicate of this subject. See Karl Marx, "Kritik der Hegelschen Staatsphilosophie (1841/1842)" in *Karl Marx: Der historische Materialismus: Die Frühschriften,* ed. S. Landshut and J. P. Mayer, in collaboration with F. Salomon (Leipzig: Alfred Kröner, 1932), I, pp. 20 ff.

> practical question. In practice, man is bound to prove the truth, that is, the reality and force, the this-worldliness of his thinking. The dispute over the reality or non-reality of his thinking isolated from practice is a pure *scholastic* question.

"The question . . . objective truth . . . is not a question of theory, but a practical question." In the second thesis, Marx transferred the question of truth from a theoretical question relating to knowing to a question of reality, the sphere of practice. How did Marx substantiate this approach? The fundamental concept around which this elucidation centers—and the fundamental concept of the first three theses—is the concept of *practice.* The question of theory arose initially in the first thesis, in which it was said that practice is revolutionary, related to the practice of critique. The meaning of critique was found to lie in measuring reality according to essence and in finding whether this essence is realized within reality. In other words, the critique measures to see whether truth exists insofar as truth—according to Hegel's definition—is the correspondence of content to itself, or the correspondence of concept to its own reality. However, the comparison of reality with its essence is not merely a theoretical comparison. Essence is not a passive or static unit. It breaks through and realizes itself within reality. Criticism restricted to the concept of truth is essentially a critique in actuality. Moreover, truth that connotes correspondence between essence and reality is not a matter determined by an onlooker; truth is bound to the very relationship between essence and reality and is connected to the very realization of essence within reality.

It can now be said that truth is bound to practice; it is bound to the same force of actualization that was raised for clarification in the first thesis. This is an interesting transformation of the concept "truth." Truth was defined classically as the correspondence between concept and reality, or, the intellect and the thing. However, the essence of this definition resulted from the stress laid on the reflective character of human knowledge, on the basis of which truth is the product of the observation of reality or is attained by reference to reality.

The classic definition was not framed to emphasize in particular the facet of practical activity. Although a change had taken place in the substance of Hegel's thinking about the content of the definition, still the definition itself was apparently firm and sound. Since the force of the idea is stressed in the idealistic position, the idea or the concept cannot be viewed as mere reflection upon given reality. In Hegel's words, nothing is real but the reasonable. Reality is not given, it is created out of reason. Marx appropriated this idea for his system. Yet, according to his program as defined in the first thesis, Marx did not stop with the abstract activity of the idea but brought into prominence the real activity of practice.

Marx's view, the main core of the dialectic, was that a continuous transition exists between man and the reality that embraces him. This transition is the work of reality and makes it possible to know this reality. The knowledge of reality from a theoretical perspective is related to the creation of reality from a practical perspective. Practice, in Marx's sense, is the guarantee that it is possible for man to know reality; in other words, because man creates reality with the strength of his being, called practice, he is likely to know this reality. (This is similar to the ideas of Giambatista Vico, the traces of which are to be found within Marx.[17]) Therefore, Marx said, the eye becomes human when its object becomes a human object, made *by* man *for* man, or a utility bereft of its mere egoistic character, turning usefulness into human usefulness. Senses become, therefore, direct and immediate, no longer theoretical. However, things take the form of objective human relationship. Marx also said that the elimination of private property will free the senses of man and their qualities, in that after the elimination of private property there will once again be no chasm between man and his reality, and the reality created by man will be his and will relate to him humanly.[18] The idea about truth when considered practically is intimately bound

[17] Stanislaw Warynski (pseud. of Leo Kofler), *Die Wissenschaft von der Gesellschaft* (Bern: A. Francke AG., 1944), p. 72.

[18] *MEGA,* I, 3, pp. 118–119; Bottomore, pp. 132–133.

to Marx's fundamental theory on the nature of practice: The practice that creates reality also creates the correspondence between essence and reality; that is, it is truth. In this view, the concept of truth was transferred from the theoretical realm to the practical; in fact—if the idea is to be analyzed at its roots—truth has no meaning in the theoretical sphere alone. The correspondence that is the essence of truth cannot be created by theory; correspondence is a creative act, an outcome of practice.

The problem of the synthesis between concept and given sense-data was central to Kant's philosophy. True empirical knowledge is the synthesis of concepts with the data presented to them through perception. Is there a guarantee, however, that the sensible datum will serve the concept that arranges it? Is there a guarantee that synthesis is possible? Hegel suggested the answer in the progressive elimination of the difference between concept and perception through the dialectical process. He viewed reality as dynamic so that the concept and the reality known through it, became identical. On this point, Marx followed the views of Hegel. But he transferred the identity of concept with reality from the realm of Spirit to the realm of reality itself, the reality created by real-sensuous practice. The identification of concept with reality takes place within the realm of reality (*Diesseits*).

Furthermore, Marx's notion of practice did not have the character of an a priori moral imperative. No distant goal stands in front of reality, directing it along its way and determining what is worth while for it. Activity is not produced by the aspiration of the present for a desired end. Activity is the product of the force of reality itself, that is, practice; it is the product of the idea that, as a practical idea, is limited to reality. Like Hegel, Marx did not urge a distinction between the present and the desired, because he viewed the dynamic force as the force of reality, not as the product of the passage from reality to the desired end beyond it.

In Marx's theory of truth found in practice, the various threads of philosophical thought from Kant to Hegel meet.

About what reality was Marx talking, however? Did he mean universal reality and with this, natural reality, or did he mean the reality of man alone, that is, history and society? This question cannot be answered from the proposition itself. The direction of dialectic thought, however, depends on its answer. Is its realm the realm of history and society, as Georg Lukács and others believed, or is its realm nature as well, as Engels believed? However, it appears from the third thesis that the view that limits the dialectic to the area of history is the correct one, in that the dialectic view is connected with the assumption of a man-created reality.

This provides a stepping stone for the clarification of the famous saying of Marx—in which programatic pronouncement can be detected—on the social existence that determines the consciousness of man.[19] Existence is the product of the process that man has made. This existence is reality not strange to man and not even strange to consciousness. Consciousness is part of the practice that creates it. Existence, the product of practice, determines consciousness; this means that consciousness is not cut off from existence and is not bound to an independent realm. Consciousness is only a part of existence, determined by its totality. The relationship between consciousness and existence is similar to the relationship between the part and the whole. But since consciousness is a part of existence and from its nature is not an element alien to it and since the whole determines its part, consciousness combined in the whole determines the consciousness that is a part of the whole.

Nevertheless, it is clear that without this proposition concerning the fundamental contiguity between man and social existence, there is no true dialectic significance to Marx's programmatic pronouncement on existence as the determinant of consciousness. Consciousness that is determined by existence without acknowledging this fact is ideological consciousness, that is to say, consciousness that represents itself as if it were

[19] Karl Marx, *A Contribution to the Critique of Political Economy,* trans. N. I. Stone from 2d German edn. (Chicago: C. H. Kerr, 1911) p. 11.

independent, yet all the while is dependent. Where there is reason for its representing itself as independent although it is only dependent, ideology serves the needs of power and dominance. (The critical analysis of this view appears in Chapter 7.)

"In practice, man is bound to prove the truth." This aspect of Marx's theory might create the impression that there is a fundamental affinity between his approach and what is known as pragmatism, or the conception of truth in pragmatism. William James's attack on rationalism would sound, from this point of view, similar to Marx's attack on idealism. William James said, for instance: "But the rationalists who talk of claim and obligation *expressly say that they have nothing to do with our practical interests or personal reasons.*" [20] Moreover, the stress on effects that might conceivably have practical bearing (Charles S. Peirce) may again create the impression that the concept of effects and the concept of practice as conceived by Marx were identical. But this is not so.

Marx's concern is practice in the sense of changing the historical reality by means of the realization of the idea of the world-history of mankind.[21] This is a world-embracing idea. Consequently, practice has as its objective the total change of reality. Pragmatism is concerned explicitly with some particular changes in our experience or with some particular consequences, because pragmatism does not begin with the total conception of reality that must be practically materialized, but with a fragmentary and piecemeal hypothesis that has to be applied to a particular experience. This leads to the notion of "functional or instrumental use in effecting the transition from a relatively conflicting experience to a relatively integrated one." [22] Taking advantage of the qualification *relatively,* it can be pointed out that Marx does not deal with a

[20] William James, *Pragmatism* (New York: Meridian Books, 1955), p. 148.

[21] *MEGA,* I, 5, p. 24.

[22] John Dewey, *Studies in Logical Theory* (Chicago: The University of Chicago Press, 1903), p. 75.

relative integration of experience, but with the full realization of an absolute idea of freedom that lacks as yet its pretended absoluteness precisely because it is not materialized within the domain of history.

Marx's theory is based on the assumption that there is a fundamental identity between man and reality. This identity may be hidden or perverted under certain circumstances. The objective of practice is to change reality in order to achieve a patent and consistent identity between man and his circumstances. Henceforth, Marx assumes that reality is rational in its core and has to be made patently so through the creation of a human society. Against this rationalistic temper can be set James's explicit statement on the empiricist leanings of pragmatism "away from . . . fixed principles, closed systems, and pretended absolutes and origins."[23] That James mentions "action" and "power" in the selfsame context should not lead us to confuse James's use of these terms with Marx's. Marx refers to principles that have to be verified by experience while creating integrated experiences.

Both these philosophies use some of the same terms but with different meanings. As it happens very often in philosophical discussion, a common term receives its specific meaning within the system itself. From this point of view, Bertrand Russell's interpretation of instrumentalism, stressing its affinity to Marx, even quoting the "Theses on Feuerbach" in a summarized form, has to be more than questioned.[24] Likewise, while Marx speaks of the realization of philosophy—in his last thesis—which implies clearly that philosophy has a defined and self-enclosed content, or substance, that has to be realized, Dewey speaks about controlling the environment and about thinking as instrumental to this task.[25] A better summary of the prag-

[23] James, p. 45; *see also* p. 167.

[24] Bertrand Russell, "Dewey's New Logic," *The Philosophy of John Dewey*, ed. Paul A. Schilpp (Evanston and Chicago: The Northwestern University Press, 1939), p. 143.

[25] John Dewey, *Essays in Experimental Logic* (Chicago: The University of Chicago Press, 1916), p. 30.

matist or instrumentalist conception of practice than Bertrand Russell's is Arthur E. Murphy's: "Intellectual inquiry is practical in that it involves making choices, manipulating materials, testing hypotheses, and so far as the inquiry is successful, changing the situation in which the investigator is doubtful into one in which his mind is at rest on the point at issue." [26] To put it briefly, Marx conceives of practice as realization, while the pragmatist theory, in its many nuances, conceives of practice as the decision as to what to do and what means to employ in the doing.

"A pure scholastic question." After having established that thinking is nothing but a part of practice, possible because of practice, again Marx found no place for the question of thinking as such, which he called, in this context, thinking "isolated from practice." A discussion involving such thinking is the product of abstraction from the true nature of thinking and practice; it is sophistication for its own sake. Hence, Marx calls such discussion, which is nothing more than argumentation, *scholastic.*

The second thesis is directed against the idealistic position that isolates theory from practice and seeks to understand theory within its own limits. The precise expression for this isolation of theory appears in the fact that it is measured by its own criterion, the criterion of truth. If truth is a feature of knowledge that isolates, then there is meaning in isolated knowledge. Hence, Marx does not attack theory as such but does attack the view that advocates the mere theoretic value of truth.

If it becomes clear that there is no autonomous determination of truth considered as a theoretical value, and that truth is necessarily bound up in practice, then isolated theory, narrowly restricted within reflective cognition, has no function. The second thesis sought to arrive at a dialectical interpretation of the relation between theory and practice.

[26] Arthur E. Murphy, "Dewey's Epistemology and Metaphysics," *The Philosophy of John Dewey,* ed. Paul A. Schilpp (Evanston and Chicago: The Northwestern University Press, 1939), p. 214.

THIRD THESIS: MAN AND CIRCUMSTANCES

> The materialistic teaching on the changing of the circumstances and education forgets that the circumstances are changed by men, and it is necessary that the educator himself be educated. This teaching, therefore, is bound to split society into two parts, of which one is superior to the other.
>
> The concurrence of changing of the circumstances and of the human activity, or self-changing, can be conceived as *revolutionary practice.*

"The materialistic teaching." In the third thesis, Marx engaged once again in an argument with materialism that he had begun in the first thesis. Although it is not referred to in the same way here as in the first thesis, in which it appeared as "all materialism up to now," it is clear that it is the same type of materialism. In Engels' edition (see Chapter 1), "Robert Owen" appeared at the end of the first paragraph of the third thesis in parentheses. Marx was probably referring to the British socialist Robert Owen (1771–1858), whose teaching provided a central position for education, and who even tried to implement his plan with the help of education.[27] But Marx's teaching need not be connected with Owen's, since French materialism, against which the critique was leveled in the first thesis, had itself maintained a central position for education.

"On the changing of the circumstances and education." What is referred to is the social offshoot of the old nondialectical materialism. It has been shown that the basis of the materialistic teaching lies in the view that reality is material, structured in accordance to mechanistic laws. Within this reality man is a machine. From this mechanistic viewpoint, materialism derived its moral outlook. Man according to his nature is

[27] Robert Owen, *A New View of Society* (Glencoe, Ill.: Free Press of Glencoe, undated, first published 1812), pp. 27, 55 ff., 66, 91.

neither good nor bad. He is a creature whom it is possible to mold, if someone will mold him. Man is formable, he is flexible like matter upon which various seals can be stamped. This flexibility is the substratum for the various directions in which it is possible to lead man. However, since man inherently and by nature lacks his own direction, its assignment must come from without. The mechanistic teaching on the essence of man, which likened him to a large clock, had to arrive at a moral-pedagogic conclusion. The clock does not set itself; it must be set from outside. Two external forces are advanced by this form of materialism: (1) the natural circumstances surrounding man and (2) those crystallized by historical conditions. These consist, on the one hand, of climate, nature, and the like, and, on the other hand, of the order of life given within society and the political regime. However, since man is formed by circumstances independent of him, in what way can he be changed? Must man necessarily follow the circumstances, which, when given, determine the path of his life forever?

If this is the condition of man, he is like a clock, which, once set, always keeps the correct time. The problem of the changing of society was not unknown to the French materialists. In the eighteenth century Helvétius and Holbach dealt extensively with it. Materialism set aside a central domain for education within the general framework of the life of society and understood education, in accordance with mechanistic suppositions, as an attempt to give direction to man. Education stamps its signature upon the flexible substratum of man's nature. It is an act the social status of which is similar to lawmaking. Legislation regulates the pattern of man's life in society by the power of exterior command, by order, government, and even by compulsion. While education has a similar function in society, it is related to the child, whereas legislation concerns itself with adult society. At any rate, this clarification of the similarity between education and legislation emphasized the mechanistic direction of materialism "up to now." [28]

[28] *See* Claude Helvétius, *De l'Esprit* (Paris: Chez Durand, 1758), last chapter; *also* Baron Paul d'Holbach, *Système Social, Ou Prin-*

"The circumstances are changed by men, and it is necessary that the educator himself be educated." Marx wished to criticize the mechanistic position. The root of his critique lies in the recognition of the impossibility of the separation of the different facets of human reality, whether we consider the separation of man from circumstances or the separation of the educator from the educated. This critique is implied in the idea of practice, which is fundamentally grounded in the awareness of the contiguity between the reality given and man who works within it. The circumstances referred to in the old materialistic view—at least the social circumstances—do not exist within an eternal, solid, and given boundary. The fitting of the circumstances to a framework of historical process renders them dynamic, that is, data that are manifestations of the dynamics of man and capable of change within the continuous dynamic power of man. Man not only brings circumstances about; he also changes them. At any rate, circumstances do not have an independent status vis-à-vis man. Whoever severs the circumstances from man behaves in accordance with the mechanism of civic (bourgeois) economy; in civic economy, where freedom, so to speak, is given to the merchandise produced by man, this merchandise becomes a power ruling over him, and finally, the fetishism of merchandise parallels the fetishism of circumstance.

In this vein, Marx wrote in *Poverty of Philosophy:* "The economists explain to us how production is carried on in the relation given, but what they do not explain is how these relations are produced, that is to say, the historical movement which has created them.[29]

"M. Proudhon, the economist, has clearly understood that men make cloth, linen, and silk-stuffs, in certain determined

cipes naturels de la moral et de la politique. Avec un examen de l'influence du gouvernement sur les moeurs (London, 1773), III, Ch. 11.

[29] Karl Marx, *The Poverty of Philosophy,* trans. H. Zwelch (Chicago: Charles H. Kerr, 1910), p. 114.

production circumstances. But what he has not understood is that these determined social circumstances are as much produced by men as the cloth, the linen, etc." [30] "Thus . . . is it not to make real profane history of the men in each century, to represent these men at the same time as the authors and the actors of their own drama?" [31] By doing this we will have returned indirectly to the same point from which we had departed. It is obvious that the reference is to the point at which Marx began himself, that is, practice.

"The concurrence of the changing of the circumstances and of the human activity, or self-changing." Marx could not separate circumstances from human activity. The entire force of his dialectical position, anchored in the realm of society, lies in the emphasis of the reciprocity between man and circumstances. The import of the dialectic consists in evincing the fact that the two facets are different from one another and yet connected in an inseparable manner. With the aid of the notion of practice, Marx attempted to explain that the relation between the circumstances and the change that comes about by the force of man's action is similar to the relation between the given and the new and to the relation between static reality and the dynamic of revolution.

This raises the problem that the critics of Marx, both socialists and nonsocialists, were eager to discuss. What is the function of revolution in a system that assumes the necessity of historical process? The origin of this critique lies in the separation between the two facets of practice; that is, its root lies in the dissolution of the dialectic tension that is the axis of Marx's system. Circumstances and revolutionary actions are the two aspects of practice. Hence, they cannot be separated. Practice creates the circumstances and changes them. Since Marx's theory is dialectic, there is no room for a first *foothold*. Practice is the first *foothold*, yet it consists by its

[30] Marx, *The Poverty of Philosophy*, p. 119.
[31] Marx, *The Poverty of Philosophy*, p. 125.

nature of two arms, as does every pair of tongs, made up of circumstances on the one hand and revolutionary change on the other. Marx does not start with a separation of circumstances from revolution, that is, a separation of thesis from antithesis, but like Hegel he starts from synthesis, or practice, whose real actualizations are thesis, on the one hand, and antithesis on the other.[32]

It is appropriate to exemplify this idea, which is of fundamental importance to the understanding of the working of the dialectic, by introducing a subject that has no bearing on Marx or on the Hegelian school. The example is drawn from the view of Wilhelm von Humbolt on language and its development. Von Humboldt said that it makes no difference if we grant to the invention process of language thousands of years: in order that man understand truthfully even one word not as an impulse of sense but as a clearly articulated sound that denotes a concept, it would be necessary that language lie entirely within him. Man is man only through language; yet in order to invent language it is first necessary to be man.[33] From Von Humboldt's pronouncement, it is possible to derive through implication the same dialectic idea met in Marx's view on practice in relation to circumstance and change.

Neither language nor man, its creator, holds any position of temporal precedence or advancement. Language creates man just as man creates language. Von Humboldt, steering clear of dialectical terminology, said that language is created spontaneously. He wanted to emphasize thereby that one cannot speak about the order and arrangement of time nor about what precedes and succeeds in time. And so it is with Marx. Circumstances condition the revolutionary practice just as the revolutionary practice qualifies the circumstances. The two

[32] On the place of the synthesis in the structure of dialectic *see* Nathan Rotenstreich, "Some Remarks on the Formal Structure of Hegel's Dialectic," *Philosophy and Phenomenological Research* Vol. V, No. 2 (December, 1944), pp. 242–254.

[33] Wilhelm von Humboldt, *Ausgewählte philosophische Schriften* (Leipzig: Felix Meiner, n.d.), p. 144.

cannot be separated even to fix the temporal antecedence of the one over the other. Production, which is—as Marx said—the first historical act, contains the characteristic tension of practice, that is, the circumstances and the change. Here we have no first foothold.

French materialism had already raised the question with which Marx was concerned, of the self-activity of man in contradistinction to the circumstances of man. Denis Diderot, in whose ideas Marx was interested, offered an answer to the question, an answer that reverberated in various forms long after. Diderot thought—presented in a literary form in *Jacques le Fatalist*—that actually man is subject to circumstances and governed by them, but in the course of acting it seems to man that he acts from his own spontaneity and strength. The dialectic between man and circumstances is actually a dialectic between reality and the illusory appearance of consciousness.[34] Marx, who grappled with the same difficulty, sought to comprehend the dialectic between man and circumstance as a true dialectic, that is, as a dialectic between two actual participants that are derived from one true and common source. The common source is the dialectic between real activity—discussed in the first thesis as sensuous activity—and the real circumstances, both being aspects of practice.

The first three theses constitute one unit, in which Marx presented his position based on the cornerstone of practice. With the help of the concept of practice, Marx expressed his synthetic view containing the sensuous aspect of materialism and the active aspect of idealism.

The first thesis introduced the central concept in its entirety. The next two theses made use of the concept of practice with respect to two problems. The first is the problem of idealism, that is, the problem of truth, and the second is the problem

[34] *See* Ernst Cassirer, *Die Philosophie der Aufklärung* (Tübingen: J. C. B. Mohr [Paul Siebeck], 1932), p. 95; *The Philosophy of the Enlightenment,* trans. Fritz Koelln and James Pettegrove (Boston: Beacon Press, 1955), pp. 71–72.

of materialism, that is, the problem of circumstances surrounding man. Practice is the synthesis of theory and action as well as of man and circumstances. The structure of the first three theses is in a way dialectic. First, Marx presented the synthesis, that is practice, and then the two positions that he viewed as antithetical with respect to his own position: idealism and materialism "up to now." In the theses that followed he dealt solely with man and society.

EXCURSUS: ROUSSEAU AND MARX

Marx was dependent on Jean Jacques Rousseau in a philosophical rather than a biographical sense, and a significant transformation occurred in the transition from Rousseau's thought to Marx's.

Mutuality. Rousseau's idea of the sovereign was in a way the cornerstone of Marx's philosophy. Rousseau said, "This public person so formed by the union of all other persons . . . is called by its members *State* when passive, *Sovereign* when active. . . . Those who are associated in it take collectively the name of *people,* and severally are called *citizens,* sharing in the sovereign power, and *subjects,* as being under the laws of the State." [35] The social contract means that man becomes his own subject; he is both law-giver and the citizen bound to the law. The sphere of the state is based on "a contract, as we may say, with himself." Thus freedom and obedience are complementary notions.

The same mutual relation is found in Marx's thought expressed in the third thesis. Man is both the producer of the conditions of his reality and subject to them; he is both the author of his drama and the actor in it. Through the revolutionizing practice, as stated in the third thesis, the two aspects of human existence—the activity and the circumstances as the given framework of that activity—can be conceived and ra-

[35] Jean Jacques Rousseau, *The Social Contract and Discourses* (London and New York: Everyman's Library, 1946), p. 13.

tionally understood. Man's sovereignty does not mean that his activity moves in a vacuum. His activity is bound to circumstances, but these circumstances are, in turn, products of the activity. The circumstances are both products and shaping factors. Thus in Marx's thought the same duality of activity and passivity is found as in Rousseau's and the same attempt to solve the problem of human freedom by stressing this complementary duality.

But here we meet with the very change that took place in the transition from Rousseau to Marx. Rousseau pointed to the duality of activity and passivity in the sphere of the state, while Marx shifted this duality to the sphere of economics and social existence. Duality for Rouseau was formal and constitutional, while for Marx it was material and sociological. The problem of freedom had a political implication for Rousseau, while this problem was essentially social for Marx. Thus the two poles of activity and passivity and their mutual relations are the common feature of Rousseau's and Marx's theories, while they differ in the spheres conjoining these poles and their interrelations. For Marx society was to occupy the place of the state, as is made clear in the tenth thesis.

Will and Practice. A parallel transformation can be found in the metabasis of *will* into *practice*. For Rousseau, man's activity was based on will. The will creates the contract. It becomes the law-giver and directs the subjects to bind themselves to the law. For Marx, man's activity appeared as practice, qua sensuous activity. Practice is the anthropological characteristic by which man distinguishes himself. Practice embodies itself *in concreto* in economic production and serves as the stimulus and as the bridge to the coming state of society. Thus Rousseau's "voluntarism" becomes "practicism." The activity ceases to be an occurrence resting on a psychological faculty and becomes one resting on a historical force. The will in Rousseau's theory creates the state, while practice in Marx's view produces history and directs it. Here, too, activism embodies itself in different spheres, and from the meaning of these spheres it gains its specific features—will and practice. Thus man's being subjected to law is an act of will, while his being subjected to circumstances is a product of history, beyond the capacity of his actual will.

Will and Norms. The main difficulty of Rousseau's theory lies, as is well known, in the problem of the rationality of the will. Rousseau tried to solve this problem by the concept of the general will. "The general will is always right . . . , there is often a great deal of difference between the will of all and the general will; the latter considers only the common interest, while the former takes private interest into account." [36] Rousseau's problem was how to guarantee the very basis of the social contract, that is, that "each man, in giving himself to all, gives himself to nobody; and there is no associate over which he does not acquire the same right as he yields others over himself, he gains an equivalent for everything he loses, and an increase of force for the preservation of what he has." [37] Through this differentiation between the will of all and the general will, Rousseau established a connection between the actual will as a psychological act and a norm that directs the act. The general will ceases to be a reality and becomes an ethical pattern. The general will as a norm becomes the guarantee that the actual will will not be fallible, that is, a selfish will that undermines the very essence and justification of the social contract.

The same interrelation between the norm of the idea and the actuality are found in Marx, but here too the interrelation becomes a sociological datum. Marx tried to discover the necessary connection between the proletariat and the idea of freedom: the particular interest of the proletariat is *ipso facto* the trend toward the realization of human freedom and sovereignty. The proletariat, on the one hand, depends on the bourgeois society and, on the other, has no place in it, because bourgeois

[36] Rousseau, pp. 22, 23.
[37] Rousseau, p. 12.

society is based on private property. This proletariat directed by its own interest becomes the bearer of human emancipation.[38] The particularity of interest and the universality of ideas are here interrelated. Thus, the norm is embodied in the actuality of an historical interest while the actuality of an interest is elevated to a normative level. In Marx's view, the difference between the will of all and the general will eventually disappears. The harmony between the interest and the idea is the guarantee of the infallibility of the interest, on the one hand, and of the materialization of the norm, on the other. One of the main difficulties of Marx's philosophy is obviously encountered here, precisely because he so closely tied up the norm with a given historical factor qua class. The detachment of the norms for Rousseau became a possible historical concretion of the norms for Marx with all the consequences following from this, including the possible and eventual consequence that the proletariat is always right, because it embodies *the* Right.

In Marx's three main points—the interdependence between activity and passivity, the concept of practice, and the harmony between the interest of the proletariat and the universal idea of freedom—we find a transformation of the concepts of Rousseau's theory. This transformation is in all its aspects a shift from the sphere of constitution and state to the sphere of history and society.

Between Marx and Rousseau lay Hegel's concept of the civil—bourgeois—society, regarded as the sphere of human reality, an activity derived from needs. Marx arrived at this point in the tenth thesis.

[38] *MEGA,* I, 3, p. 207.

CHAPTER 4

Theses on Man and Society

FOURTH THESIS: RELIGION AND ITS REAL FOUNDATIONS

> Feuerbach starts out from the fact of religious self-alienation, of duplication of the world into a religious and into a worldly one. His work consists in resolving the religious world into its worldly substratum. But that the worldly substratum sets itself apart from itself and fixes itself in an independent (nebulous) realm, can be explained only by the self-discord and self-contradiction of this worldly substratum. Therefore, the latter, in itself, as well as in its contradiction, must be understood and practically revolutionized. Hence, for example, once the earthly family is disclosed as the secret of the holy family, the former must now be annihilated both theoretically and practically.

"Feuerbach starts out from the fact of religious self-alienation." Marx summarized the main points of Feuerbach's position on the essence of religion. Marx did not disagree with Feuerbach's view, and—as pointed out in Chapter 1—he took his own view on religion from Feuerbach. Marx also agreed with the conclusion Feuerbach drew as to the nature of religion, looking at religion as reflecting the nature of man. Yet, Marx attempted to continue the critical line that Feuerbach had introduced and to disclose the roots of religion in the reality of society.

"Can be explained only by the self-discord and self-contradiction of this worldly substratum." Marx placed at the center

of his critical approach to the essence of religion the inquiry into the real foundations of religion, that is, the inquiry into man. Feuerbach himself believed that the root of the development of religion is bound in the contradiction existing between real man and the ideal to which he aspires. This contradiction finds expression in desire or yearning. Hence, Feuerbach said that God is the yearning inexpressible, stamped in the depths of the soul of man.

Marx attempted to clarify this inner contradiction in man. His question was: Why does man reach religious self-alienation at all? Why does he split himself? The main answer is that human reality as such is split, since human essence is unrealized, and man is enslaved to himself and to the products of his hands. The fundamental problem is, therefore, the problem of the elimination of the contradiction within reality, and the elimination of religion is determined, *ipso facto,* by the elimination of the root that nourishes it. Religion is an imaginary realization of human essence, and man is dependent upon this realization because his essence has not reached as yet its true reality. Since his essence is unrealized, man sees in the entities of religion the sun around which he revolves. But this sun is an imaginary one, as long as man does not rotate around his own axis. Marx set out to transfer religion from its self-contained realm to the realm that is the backbone of its creation, i.e., actual society. He argued against Feuerbach in "German Ideology" that he did not recognize the relation between society and religion and that the aspect of politics is missing in Feuerbach's critique. (It is interesting to note that Marx referred to the first criticism in his letter to Arnold Ruge.) Marx argued against Feuerbach that the dismissal of religion, or the elimination of religious consciousness and its exchange for the consciousness of man and for the ideal perfection of his human species—even if the perfection will not be substantialized in a divine existence—will not affect the essential human reality in which man is settled. In overtly sarcastic language, Marx argued that when Feuerbach sees a man struck with sickness he pins his hopes on the consciousness of the whole human race. The man struck with sickness supposedly finds comfort in the consciousness that the human race as such does not have the flaws prevailing in his individual being. Furthermore, Marx said the practical materialist will change the industry and the structure of society that breed the sickness of men who live in their midst.[1]

Since Feuerbach and Marx agreed on the essence of religion, the acute point in their debate was the approach to be employed in eliminating religion. Feuerbach advocated that man know the human origin of religion, for this very knowledge will elucidate the nature of religion. The divine world is a human world. Marx urged that the knowledge of the true origin of religion and hence a change in consciousness is not enough. He wanted a change in reality, his fundamental assumption being that a changed reality, from which disjunction and contradiction are absent, will no longer breed religion.

Marx also gave indications of another view on the elimination of religion. In the "Paris Manuscripts" frequently relied on for the purpose of understanding his principal ideas, Marx said that for the socialistic man, he who creates history as well as himself, there will no longer be any place for religion, for religion sees man as created by an exterior or transcendent sovereignty. The position that man is dependent upon an exterior sovereignty is still contained in the view that man has not yet arrived at any discovery of his true essence. This position still limits man to something nonessential. On the other hand, the main point of the concept of practice lies in the teaching that man creates his own existence. Marx felt that this was the great idea of Hegel's *The Phenomenology of the Spirit.* By its very nature it removes the foundation from religion, for man stays confined in his inner world without need of a creating force or a creator from without. Therefore, Marx said—and it is obvious that this was based on Feuerbach—the socialist no longer has to have an intermediary or has to

[1] *MEGA,* I, 5, p. 34; Karl Marx and Friedrich Engels, *The German Ideology,* trans. and ed., with introduction, by R. Pascal (New York: International Publishers, 1947), p. 37.

negate God in order to affirm man. The socialist establishes his starting point in the sensuous consciousness of man that is simultaneously theoretical and practical. From this point, he sets out to understand the human historical process. The consciousness of the socialist is not the negative product of religious consciousness, but it is a positive consciousness that is created by the positive life of man.[2]

The approach to the essence of religion moved Marx to a critique of society, which itself engenders religion. Practice frees man from dependence on religion in that it makes man autonomous. Practice is the tool for the elimination of religion; in the context of practice, religion will no longer grow. It is evident that in this theory Marx assumed that the essence of religion was in the creation and in the dependence of man upon the creator.

"The earthly family is disclosed as the secret of the holy family." Here Marx carried on Feuerbach's idea. The "holy family" is the Holy Trinity in the Christian outlook: The concept of the Father, the Son, and the Holy Ghost is of necessity an idealistic-imaginative reflection of the real family of man on earth, according to the principle that the divine world is an ideal, projected form of the human world. Feuerbach did not give such an explanation of the origin of the Christian view of the Trinity. He did not ascribe the Divine Trinity to the human trinity, nor is there even a complete parallelism: on one side, Father, Son and Holy Ghost; on the other, father, mother, and son. However, Feuerbach refers to this view when he likens God to the "ego," the Son to "you," and the Holy Ghost to the "binding love" between the two. Feuerbach sought to explain the religious world in terms of the human world, as Marx understood him, that is, in terms of the relation between man and his fellow man, and the

[2] *MEGA,* I, 3, pp. 125–126; Karl Marx, "Economic and Philosophical Manuscripts," trans. T. B. Bottomore, in Erich Fromm, *Marx's Concept of Man* (New York: Frederick Ungar, 1961), pp. 129–130.

love that creates the unity between them. Marx assigned to the religious realm a more distinct sociological significance. He started from the organized social unit, that is, the family. And it is no mere coincidence that Feuerbach held to his general anthropological outlook; whereas Marx, who sought to understand religion through its social background, apprehended religion in its actual social reality, through the reality of the family. In brief, Marx adhered in this thesis to the teachings of Feuerbach as to the essence of religion. He, too, holds the idea of self-alienation (analyzed in Chapter 7).

"Be annihilated both theoretically and practically." Theoretically, the human origin of religion can be known as Feuerbach knew it. But beyond this the actual social background of the development of religion must be understood. Practically, practical-social conclusions must be drawn from the theoretical knowledge that has been acquired. Theory must nourish practice, and practice must confirm the adequacy of theory. Practice must actualize the conclusion at which theory has arrived.

FIFTH THESIS: PERCEPTION AND ACTION

> Feuerbach, not satisfied with *abstract thinking,* advocates perception; but he does not conceive sensibility as *practical* human-sensuous activity.

In order to confirm once again the reciprocal relationship between theory and practice, Marx went back to the starting point of the entire elucidation. He insisted upon the distinction between himself and Feuerbach: Feuerbach remained in the realm of theory, and, therefore, his approach to the world and to reality is one of reflection. The difference between Feuerbach and theoretical idealism lay in Feuerbach's making perception a tool of reflection; idealism relied on thinking while Feuerbach relied on perception. Marx transferred the discussion from the domain of reflection to the domain of practice, and herein also lay the difference between Feuerbach and Marx in their respective relations to religion and the conclusions inferred from its critique.

SIXTH THESIS: THE HUMAN SPECIES AND SOCIETY

> Feuerbach resolves the religious essence into the *human* essence. But the human essence is not an abstract, inherent in the single individual. In its reality it is the ensemble of the social conditions.
>
> Feuerbach does not go into the criticism of this real essence and is, therefore, compelled (1) to abstract from the historical course of events, to fix a religious mental disposition, and to presume an abstract—*isolated*—human individual; (2) the essence can therefore be conceived only as "species," as inward, mute generality, binding the many individuals *naturally*.

"The human essence is not an abstract, inherent in the single individual. In its reality it is the ensemble of the social conditions." In the sixth thesis the analysis deals with the position of society in the life of man, and Marx brought the discussion to bear not on the essence of religion but on the question of the character of society.

Marx argued against Feuerbach that the latter did not consider the human essence as being manifested in society, but as inherent in the individual. Marx argued that the starting point in Feuerbach's system is the individual and not society. Yet in the "Paris Manuscripts," Marx recapitulated Feuerbach's contribution to human thought by saying that it was the projection of sociability, giving this the position of a fundamental principle of Feuerbach's theory.[3] Why did Marx argue against Feuerbach that his point of departure was the individual and not sociability?

It was made clear in Chapter 1 that Feuerbach saw reality as a relationship existing between the "I" and "Thou" and in the love binding the two. Man is inherently a comrade, bound to his fellow man. In this connection, which is essentially a

[3] *MEGA,* I, 3, p. 152; Bottomore, p. 170.

relationship between individuals of different sexes, Feuerbach saw the embodiment of the true dialectic. Herein a connection or unity occurs between different components. How did this arch-idea of Feuerbach escape Marx's attention and how did he argue that Feuerbach based his theory on the individual? A more fundamental examination of the matter will either justify Marx's argument or at least explain its basis. The relationship within which Feuerbach saw the social relation and the essence of human reality is the intimate relation between people, that is, a limited social relation. This intimate relation occurs because of the essentially sensual bond of love within the realm of nature. According to Feuerbach, sociability means intimate living expressed through the bonds of love, and it does not mean social life carried on in the historical course of events. This is one of the causes for the argument between Feuerbach and Marx. Where is society located? Is it within this framework, is it in nature and consolidated upon such a natural basis as love; or is it in history and consolidated upon a social-historical basis? Marx transferred sociability from its intimate status to an objective realm, and, in this case, from the realm of love as a natural relation to the realm of society as a domain of social significance.

Feuerbach elucidated the essence of religion, which, in accordance with his fundamental assumption, reflects the essence of man. He did this through an analysis of the quality of human consciousness. The essence of human consciousness is that it spreads beyond the limits of ego and refers to fellow human beings or to the human species as a whole.

Consciousness is the consciousness of the individual, but through it the individual is bound to his species and to members of his species. Society is not a primary datum, from which we set out to clarify the direction and essence of human reality; here society appears as species, given by means of consciousness, whereas consciousness is the quality of the individual. Therefore, the relationship to society is not direct. It takes place through the mediation of consciousness, which is the quality of the individual. If this is so, two concentric circles can be drawn in Feuerbach's system. The inner circle is limited to the bond between "I" and "Thou" and the larger circle–the relationship between man and his species–is a relationship by means of consciousness. However, if human essence is an essence of species, it does not appear in the life of the individual as an active factor, but merely as an object of reflective consciousness. We return again to the starting point of the argument between Feuerbach and Marx. Are we bound in the realm of consciousness, or are we bound in reality, that is, in activity?

"Feuerbach does not go into the criticism of this real essence." Because Feuerbach apprehended human essence as intimately or consciously given, he did not regard it as a dynamic reality to which criticism applies, as did Marx, according to whom criticism scrutinized reality. Human essence was perceived by Feuerbach as an ultimate datum, beyond which there is nothing, whether it materializes itself in intimate togetherness, making it the fundamental cell of human life, or whether it is perceived as an object of consciousness as the absolute supplementation of the flaws man sees and knows in his real life. In either case, human essence is not an historical reality, because either it is an intimate but nonhistorical and nonobjective reality, or it is not a reality at all, but only an object of consciousness.

"Compelled to abstract from the historical course of events." Feuerbach completely severed sociability from history. He removed sociability's dynamic aspect, and thereby no longer viewed society as the autonomous constructive force of man—practice. The abstraction from the course of history also abstracts from the practice of man.

"Compelled . . . to fix a religious mental disposition." Because Feuerbach did not ground his discussion of man in history, he could not apprehend the essence of religion from the standpoint of the social-historical development of man. Feuerbach

necessarily arrived at a psychological interpretation of the essence of religion, that is, he aimed to discover the constant emotional elements that are the basis of religion. The severance of emotional factors from the objective-social realm was described by Marx, in accordance with a terminological reference of Feuerbach's, as the assumption of an independent mental-religious disposition. Marx, as demonstrated in the fourth thesis, urges a clarification of the essence of religion through an analysis of society, not through a reliance on the emotional factors given in the personality of man. Therefore, Marx argued that religion is sustained by historical forces and societal changes, but not by constant emotional forces.

"Human individual." Because for Feuerbach religion was connected with consciousness and its structure, it is connected with the individual. To return to the starting point of the argument, Feuerbach posited the individual as the ultimate datum. Marx argued against him that he posited the *isolated* individual. Following Hegel, Marx called every isolated "given" abstract, for the basis of abstraction for Hegel was in the severing of a part or member from the whole. "Isolated" means "abstract," whereas "the whole" means "the concrete," the contrary of the abstract.

"The [human] essence . . . as 'species.'" Feuerbach used the word "species" when he spoke about the consciousness of species and about religion, which reflects the species-consciousness of man. The concept of species can be understood in two ways: either logically or biologically. In the logical sense, species means the sum total of characteristics used by the classifier to indicate the combination of particulars in a generic unit. The concept of species in the natural sciences (biology) may be understood similarly. The species of certain living creatures is not real as such; it is an abstract entity designed to embrace the various elements. A species does not exist in reality but only nominally. The concept of species

when marking the collective life of man, does away with it, since it transforms it from an active reality into a collection of characteristics for the mere purpose of logical or scientific classification.

However, Marx's basic argument was stated from a different standpoint. That the concept of species is basic in biology —species of mammals, reptiles, etc.—caused Marx to object. Society is apt to be understood as a fact of nature with all of its implications, and first and foremost as an immutable given, and then, we only return to where we started. Then species would be a natural, not a historical, fact, apprehended as an ultimate fact to which the critique, when linked to revolutionary practice, could not apply. "Feuerbach's whole deduction with regard to the relation of one man to another, goes only to prove that men need and always have needed each other. He wants to establish consciousness of this fact, that is to say, like the other theorists to produce a correct consciousness about an existing fact. Whereas for the real communist it is a question of overthrowing the existing state of things,"[4] Marx said in "German Ideology." Marx insisted on the internal relationship between the views regarding society as a historical reality and those regarding society as a dynamic unit, given to flux and revolutionary change. The view that regards society as a natural reality implies that it is a given reality; and if society is viewed as a historical reality, the implication is that it is changeable and capable of converting itself. Therefore, the viewpoints of Marx and Feuerbach can be distinguished on the question of the nature and place of consciousness. Feuerbach began his analysis with consciousness and finished with an elucidation of the relationship between man and his species; whereas Marx, as will be discussed further under the seventh thesis, saw consciousness as an event within society and not as a primary datum. Language, Marx said, and even consciousness was created out of the need of man to come into contact with his fellow man. Consciousness is in its essence

[4] *MEGA,* I, 5, p. 31; Pascal, p. 33.

a product of society, and it will continue as long as man continues to exist.[5] This view is merely another expression of the theory of the determination of consciousness by reality, which is here interpreted to mean social reality. It has been shown already that the basis for the idea lies in the primary nature of practice, the creator of social reality and the determining factor of consciousness accompanying this creation. It is clear that Marx did not ascribe the genesis of society to consciousness, but saw it as the product of man's relation to society.

With this explanation of the nature of the Marxian critique of Feuerbach's concept of society, some of the main points in Marx's positive attitude toward the nature of society can be delineated, thereby further explaining the critique leveled by Marx. Let us consider them in turn.

"What" and "How" of production. The nature of individuals is determined not only by *what* they produce, but also by *how* they produce.[6] Marx held that human reality is not determined by a constant number of products, at the foundation of which lies some natural-given base. Human reality is also determined by the "how," which changes and is fitted to the technical framework created by man himself. Not only that, but man is the one who determines the "what," that is, the quality of the goods of man and the articles that provide for these goods.

Two aspects of this idea must be stressed. Man's image is necessarily determined not only by the given needs, but also by the means for responding to these needs. The system of means is a technical-historical complex. It is not given; it is created or produced by man. From this point of view, human society is a society of men building together the means for supplying their needs. Even their needs are not given, however. They enter a dynamic framework and are directed by it. When viewed as a social reality, human reality is dy-

[5] *MEGA,* I, 5, p. 20; Pascal, pp. 19 ff.
[6] *MEGA,* I, 5, pp. 5 ff.; Pascal, pp. 19 ff.

namic. It is created by man and not independent of any foundation related to man.

Marx again returned to his first thought, wherein he attempted to apprehend society as an autonomous reality, that is, as a reality built upon a real social basis, and not upon, on the one hand, biological, or, on the other, mental, foundations. Any attempt to explain the nature of society as a stage in the evolution of nature is rejected on principle, because any such attempt eliminates the irreducible nature of society—its autonomous creation—and makes society dependent upon presocietal or postsocietal factors. This also holds true in such attempts as that of Feuerbach to build a social sphere out of our desires and affections for our fellow men. The dialectical view in matters of society implies that society is an autonomous unit, that is, constructed upon a social foundation, implying the conquest and humanization of nature, and not upon such natural instincts as gregariousness.

The motive that brought Marx to the discovery of the unique social position of human reality in economics, in its primary deterministic sense, can now be clarified. Economics (in Marx's terms, economic production) is the first historical act, since it is in economics that men by their own action supply their natural needs. Economics is the bridge between nature and history, or, metaphorically, it is the wheelbarrow in which nature is moved and becomes history. Therefore, economics and the economic product determine the distinction between man and animal. The animal obtains its means of subsistence from what is around it and ready, whereas man creates these means. Man adapts—Marx's expression—nature as a framework of given factors to the power of his activity, that is, to social activity. The supposition that society is a dynamic reality and therefore unnatural relates to the point from which Marx's theory issues, the idea of practice. The combination of society and practice prepares the ground for the dialectical understanding of society as a self-constructing entity.

Circumstances and Generations. It is instructive to see how Marx fitted his view of the relation of man to circumstances to this position on the dynamic character of society. Prevalent in every stage of history is a material sum-total of the forces of production. This sum-total is a relationship to nature created historically by men and passed on to each new generation by its predecessor. This material condensation of the productive forces of property and of circumstances—in which change implemented by the preceding generation takes place —also prescribes its way of life to the future generation and determines its character.[7] Marx, in his conceptual language, already familiar from the third thesis, summarized this idea, urging that the circumstances determine man, just as man determines the circumstances. This matter is of utmost importance since it contains the synthesis of two ideas: the rhythm of the movement between man and the circumstances of his life and the rhythm of the movement between the generations. The rhythm between man and circumstances, a social rhythm, is also the rhythm between generations. The social rhythm is basically a historical rhythm, and the dynamics of society and its historicity are of the same nature.

Objects and Society. The main point is reflected in a third line of thought, however. The point can be elucidated by a question, the tone of which is supposedly primitive in function, and therefore unsuitable, as it were, to Marxian suppositions. What does society give or grant man? Marx regarded as "impudence" the view that attempts to make man into man. The Marxian reply is encountered in his view on the position of society: Society gives all. Actually, Marx made the two concepts, human and social, identical. He said that man is socially active in so far as he is active as man.[8] Social man is a human man.[9] How does Marx define humanity, therefore,

[7] *MEGA,* I, 5, p. 34–35; Pascal, p. 38.
[8] *MEGA,* I, 3, pp. 115–116; Bottomore, p. 129.
[9] *MEGA,* I, 3, p. 114: Bottomore, p. 127.

and how does this definition correspond to society? Man is not swallowed up by the objects that he himself creates, according to Marx, if these objects are objects of society.[10] The identification of man as subject with objects-of-man and with goods as objects, is possible in reference to society. Individual man—so this idea must be understood—is incapable of arriving at control over his goods. He is likely to be dependent upon and enslaved to goods and to commodities even though he himself creates them. Only when the ownership passes to the public sphere can man rise to the level of man, that is, as a creature who is not enslaved to circumstances or to objects. Then, and only then, is the identification of man with objects created and accomplished. Society on which the powers and the means of production are based, a society that is thus the medium of human existence, is the only means for the realization of the freedom of man from the fetishism of commodity. Only in society can man reach a level of sovereignty in his life; only here does man become free. The central position of society in Marx's theory is dependent upon the fact that it is the very sphere in which the essential freedom of man is realized.

It is appropriate to note again, in the context of this idea, the comparison of Marx with Rousseau. In Rousseau's doctrine, the problem of the sovereignty of man was already central. As a solution of the problem a social contract was suggested in which man was not subjected to his fellow man but to himself. Freedom was interpreted negatively by Rousseau as disobedience to one's fellow man and positively as obedience of man to himself. The problem of freedom or sovereignty was discussed by Rousseau when dealing with the relationship between man and his fellow man, which in itself created the social or political relationship. Marx, on the other hand, transferred the problem from the relationship of man to his fellow man, to the control by man of nature, or the relationship between man and the circumstances surrounding him. The content of the concept of sovereignty has not

[10] *MEGA,* I, 3, p. 119; Bottomore, p. 133.

changed, that is, the lack of subjection to one's fellow man or the obedience of man to himself. However, Marx revealed that even when man is not subjected to man, he may be subjected to a commodity, which is a mere product of the practice of man. Therefore, Marx urged the attachment of the freedom present in the relationship between man and his products, finding that without this freedom neither is there reality in the freedom present in the relationship between man and his fellow man. Freedom or sovereignty in the relationship between man and his fellow man is an imaginary freedom, as long as man is enslaved to nonhuman goods. Man who is obedient to himself is a human being; however, for this reason, it is necessary that objects be humanized. Society as dynamic reality is destined to a central position in Marx's theory, because it is necessary to apprehend society in its dynamic nature if this realization is to take place; that is, it must be regarded in the area of history and not in the area of nature.

SEVENTH THESIS: DEPENDENCE ON SOCIETY

> Feuerbach does not see, therefore, that "the religious mental disposition" itself is a social product and that the abstract individuum, whom he analyzes, belongs to a particular form of society.

"Religious mental disposition." The seventh thesis again summarizes the basic idea posited in the previous thesis. The disposition Marx refers to is the consciousness of man as reflected in religion. The reliance on consciousness for the explanation of the essence of religion, characteristic of Feuerbach's viewpoint, is interpreted as reliance on "the religious mental disposition." Just as Marx believed consciousness to be a social product, similarly, he held that the religious disposition, as a conscious state, is a social product. And since consciousness as the quality of the individual is the product of society, the individual conscious man is a social product. Marx defined the relationship between the individual and society by characterizing the individual as the subjective existence of society,

society as thought and experienced.[11] In this, Marx indicated that from the point of view of the contents of individual existence, these contents are those of the society in which man lives; society determines the individual, that is, existence determines consciousness. Yet, the totality of society lies—ideally—in the realm of the individual. Society, via the individual, is thus given a subjective existence, or it acquires for itself through the individual a reflective existence. Ideal totality, or subjective existence, thus means consciousness. The difference between society and the individual is not a difference of contents. The difference is in the quality of the connection with consciousnes, such that the individual who possesses consciousness knows consciously of contents that are his. To use Hegel's terminology, it seems permissible to say that the difference between the individual and society is like the difference between the subjective and the objective Spirit. For Hegel, objective Spirit is the entirety of what is given in society and history; whereas subjective Spirit is the complex of the levels of consciousness. Marx, however, derives subjective Spirit from objective Spirit. In other words, consciousness emerges through the complex of the given contents, or the individual emerges from society. Still, it is unclear whether Marx believed that only the contents of consciousness emerge from society, or whether the fact of consciousness so emerges. However, it can be assumed that Marx thought it was the *contents* that are determined. (This topic is considered below in Chapter 6.)

The discussion about the dependence of the individual on society and about man as the possessor of consciousness or subjective existence throws new light on the programmatic dictum that consciousness is determined by existence. It can now be said that the determination of consciousness by existence means that (the contents of) society determines the individual. Furthermore, existence establishes consciousness, and society establishes the individual, for, as shown before, they are identical in terms of contents. The individual is identical with

[11] *MEGA*, I, 3, p. 117; Bottomore, pp. 130–131.

society. However, according to Marx, society is a historical reality and henceforth not a natural and immutable reality. Therefore, Marx became quite precise in the present thesis, and spoke about the specific form of society in order to emphasize the dynamic-historical quality of society. Society does not denote the human species in the biological sense of the term. It is a historical society and thus a specific form of social existence, since within history only specific phenomena are encountered.

EIGHTH THESIS: PRACTICE AND ITS PERCEPTION

> All social life is essentially *practical.* All mysteries that induce theory to mysticism find their rational solution in human practice and in the conception of this practice.

"All social life is . . . practical." This summarizes concisely what was elucidated in the first thesis, raised in the second and third theses, and emphasized again in the fifth.

"Mysticism." Marx's use of the term "mysticism," or its root in such forms as "mystification," was frequent. Marx used the term's popular meaning to indicate the vagueness of abstract theory. Mysticism or mystification is the creation of an abstract theoretical sphere, cut off from reality and practice, concealing reality, and then establishing a gap between theory and reality. The principal aspect of the critique of this view was discussed under the second thesis.

"Their . . . solution in . . . practice and in the conception of this practice." Marx illustrated the two sides of his view: the practical side, in the narrow meaning of the concept practice, and the theoretical side, attached to the practical. Hence he spoke about practice and its conception. Consciousness accompanies the objective reality of practice. The combination of objective practice and its consciousness is the key, by means of which Marx tried to solve various problems and to eliminate

the imaginative reality of abstract theory; theory should be connected to practice and hence unseverable from it.

The emphasis on the theoretical aspect of consciousness stressed by the word "conception" is perhaps the foothold for the distinction Marx made between the given objective existence of the social sphere and its conscious existence. When a particular social class reaches the level of conscious reality, it becomes an active subject of political and social struggle. This emphasis was also dealt with in the discussion of the seventh thesis, on the relation of man to society.

CHAPTER 5

Theses on Social Theory

NINTH THESIS: OLD MATERIALISM AND ITS SOCIAL THEORY

> The highest that perception-materialism reaches, that is, the materialism that does not conceive of sensibility as practical activity, is the perception of the single individuals in the civil society.

"Perception-materialism" is the materialism "up to now" that Marx discussed in the first and third theses. The third thesis deals with the social manifestation of this materialism, the relation between man and circumstances and the place of education in this context. In the ninth thesis, Marx took a decisive step by revealing the essential connection between the materialism "up to now" and society as it is.

"Perception of individuals." Materialism "up to now" was related to an atomistic view of social life, in that its departure point rested in the separate existence of the single individuals. Society is the product of the organization of individuals, and even this organization is founded on egoistic motives. French materialism had described the matter in this way, especially Helvétius, who said in *De l'homme* that interest and want are the principles of sociability. Now Marx turned his analysis to the egoistic and utilitarian views of the materialism "up to

now." He sought to understand the connection between materialism as a theory, turning upon the explanation of the structure of the world, and the egoistic theory of morals, pointing to the essential connection between the world view and the ethical theory. Since the old materialism analyzed the given and not the dynamic, it apprehended the world as a given material structure and society as an egoistic framework of individuals, organizing themselves in order to maintain what is theirs. Marx argued that there exists an essential connection, on the one hand, between perception and egoism and, on the other, between activity and real sociability.

"Civil society." [1] The concept of civil society was already prevalent in the thinking of the generations preceding Marx. Hobbes—whose view of social life was "mechanistic"—had used it and so also had Rousseau; it was related in this context to the distinction between the state of nature and the political state. However, it is clear that when Marx spoke about civil society he referred to the theory crystallized by Hegel; Marx dealt with this at length in his early writings. It is therefore necessary to connect what Marx said in explaining the content of the concept civil society and that to be found in Hegel concerning public life.

Speaking of the essence of civil society, Marx said that, "Civil society embraces the whole material intercourse or individuals within a specific stage in the development of the productive forces." [2] The individual who appears in civil society is an egoistic individual. He regards himself basically as an atom without any relationship.[3] Civil society is not an

[1] Following T. M. Knox's *Philosophy of Right,* the German *"bürgerlich"* is here rendered as "civil." Yet in the explanation, the term "bourgeois" is also used. Employment of the term "civil" maintains the continuity from Hegel to Marx that comes to the fore in Marx's early notes on his *Kritik der Hegelschen Staatsphilosophie.*

[2] *MEGA,* I, 5, p. 25; Pascal, p. 26.

[3] *MEGA,* I, 3, p. 296.

eternal form of life; it develops along with the bourgeoisie.[4] It appears from the foregoing that Marx saw civil society as a material-economic sphere, built upon the existence of individuals each desiring to maintain his own in the sphere of general contact and exchange. The two lines of thought on the essence of civil society—the egoistically self-contained character of the individual and the external relationship that he has with other individuals by way of give-and-take—reached Marx through Hegel's description and clarification of the character of this society.

Hegel saw public life as constructed on three levels, or in three areas: family, civil society, and the state. Civil society as an intermediate stage between the family and the state is an economic-material stage defined as a system of needs. At this stage, man is limited in that he is a creature having material needs who produces in order to satisfy these needs. Hegel discussed these aspects of the character of civil society: As mentioned above, (1) needs define the nature of society and its place within human reality. Man because of his economic nature has common economic interests with other men. The coming together of these of differing interests creates (2) the economic-social classes or estates (*Stände*)—the place and function of the police force in civil society is here passed over intentionally. Civil society as an economic-material domain, founded upon a system of needs of man, is an area of competition and struggle, demonstrating that a framework of needs does not suffice. This competition is protected by (3) laws as a protection of property, lest it be expropriated; that is, the legislative measures are a deterrent to competition. Competition itself creates the organizing activities of man, which are not essential, being an organization constructed upon an economic basis only.[5]

[4] Karl Marx, *Karl Marx: Der historische Materialismus: die Frühschriften,* ed. S. Landshut and J. P. Mayer (Leipzig: F. Kröner, 1932), I, p. 26.

[5] Georg Hegel, *Grundlinien der Philosophie des Rechts* (2d edn.; Leipzig: Felix Meiner, 1921), pp. 158–159; Hegel, *Philosophy of*

Hegel regarded man in civil society as limited to a domain of split morality. The significance of this term is clarified by a concise tracing of the position of the family in Hegel's theory of public life. Hegel did not regard the family as the cell of a struggle for survival. He regarded it as a cell of patterns and ways of life that bind the members of a family into a close framework, with a certain manner and character of its own. Hegel viewed the family as a form of immediate morality, in which no man behaves in accordance with a conscious command or with an idea that he adjusts himself to consciously. Man is immersed in the family in a naïve manner or in an immediate way of living. But man, as a creature fighting for material existence, goes beyond the confines of his family, and comes into material contact with those of similar and opposing interests. Thus he creates a second sphere for himself, built, not on his being attached to a way of life, but on a dynamic struggle for existence. Man in civil society is engaged, therefore, in a sphere of ethical dissolution.[6] And now, a third area of man's life in society emerges: the state. In the state man outgrows his struggle for existence and becomes a free man living in an objective realm wherein the realization of the ethical idea takes place. As such, the state is the domain of perfect morality. Yet in the state, man does not live his life simply or traditionally in keeping with customary modes of behavior. Man lives in accordance with the idea, and consciously so. The state is like civil society. It is an objective sphere, unlike the narrow sphere of the members of a household. Yet, in contradistinction to civil society, it is not a sphere wherein a struggle for existence and competition occurs, but a quiescent and final domain wherein the realization of the moral idea is achieved.

In the ninth thesis, Marx attempted to show that the moral theory proceeding from the egoistic character of man is the

---

Right, trans. T. M. Knox (Oxford: The Clarendon Press, 1942), p. 126.

[6] Hegel, *Grundlinien der Philosophie des Rechts,* pp. 153 ff.; Hegel, *Philosophy of Right,* pp. 122 f.

theory of the old materialism. It must of necessity treat the organization of men not as a real society, but as a combination of individuals, connected one to another in their mutual affairs within the economic sphere of give-and-take. The old materialism had thus attached itself to the existing reality of society. Insofar as it is a social theory, it reaches the existing society. Yet, Marx hoped to achieve a meeting between the active aspect of practical materialism and the new theory of the essence of society. The tenth thesis refers to this issue. Moreover, he argued that Hegel and his followers, who obviously could not be considered materialistic, adopted its description of society from materialism. Hegel then proceeded toward a higher level of moral life beyond bourgeois or civil society.

TENTH THESIS: HUMAN SOCIETY

> The standpoint of the old materialism is the civil society; the standpoint of the new, the human society or social humanity.

In contradistinction to civil society Marx posited human society. What is the meaning of the term "human" when it is linked with the term "society"? It has been pointed out above that Marx identified human activity with social activity; human activity implied for Marx a social relationship in which man was not swallowed up in the world of objects. With this tenth thesis, human society, or social humanity, was made the opposite of civil, or bourgeois, society. Marx was aware of the inner relationship between the struggle for existence and the competition that denotes civil society and the social life that engulfs man in the world of commodities that he himself creates. The struggle for existence and competition exist only in a society where there is a clash of interests between society itself and its members. It exists in a society in which man sells his working power. Social humanity, a society whose conditions of life are human, does away with the causes of the struggle for economic existence and the dependency of

straction (state and freedom), on the other. The relevant issue in the debate with Hegel was on this point, which also corresponded to the question about the essence of the dialectic: Hegel could conceive of history as reaching its self-expression in a point of satiation, for he argued that man was bound in two domains at once and that the synthesis of these domains created the climax of human history. Freedom, according to Hegel, is materialized for it is of the very nature of the state. The dialectical tension, as it were, necessitates this situation. For the state, in which the civil society is situated, is a society of egoistic individuals who dominate one another and defend themselves by laws and/or by a police force. Hegel's dialectical theory on this matter is a hierarchical theory. The state is not a comprehensive reality, including all aspects of man's life; rather, it is the supreme stage of man's life surpassing all other stages that differ from it in their position and contents. Marx, on the other hand, does not hold such a hierarchical view concerning public and historical life—a view that maintains that various levels of human existence, such as the competing bourgeois society and the state, exist side by side; and that existence maintains them in their nonrational separation.

Taking a position in which socialism is born, as becomes clear in the last thesis, Marx advocated a comprehensive framework in which all the aspects of human life are assimilated and the moral idea qua freedom is realized. The comprehensive sphere is not the state, but society. Marx, therefore, proposed to place the state on its real basis, relating it to the actual life of human beings, and to substitute society for the state. However, this will not be a bourgeois society, but a free society. Such a society must become a human society or social humanity, a society identical with a living framework that is not subordinated to a set of objects created by itself. In the discussion of this problem, therefore, all the lines of Marx's thought meet. As against the abstract reality of the state, he posits the concrete reality of society; as against the synthesis of public life, which maintains the actual dichotomy of this life, he posits the historical realization of a new form of life. This form does not sustain the old structure but introduces a real structure of life, the human society, identical with the socialist society. In this context, the motif of concreteness operating against idealism (in the first thesis) corresponds to the motif of historicity exercised against the old materialism and especially against Feuerbach (in the sixth and seventh theses).

The principal argument of Marx against Hegel's theory of public life, an argument at whose base rests a new theory of historical life, has been outlined, as well as the nature of the dialectic synthesis. Marx's second argument, an empirical rather than an a priori argument, attempted to evince that in historical reality as it exists no state is placed above bourgeois society, which thus becomes allegedly the reality of the moral idea, as Hegel viewed it.

Bourgeoisie. In Marx's definition and description of the essence of bourgeois society, he pointed out the connection between bourgeois society and the reality of the social class of bourgeoisie. Marx regarded Hegel's theory, which raises the state beyond the occurrences of real life taking place in bourgeois society, as an innovation of modern times, a historical period specifically connected with the rise of the bourgeoisie. Only in the modern period does this characteristic double severance occur: seemingly the state cuts itself off from real life, just as private life cuts itself off from public life. The Greek *polis* was a comprehensive social reality in which there was no place for a separation between state and society, not even between the state and the private sphere of the individual. Hence, according to Marx, Hegel's theory did not reflect an essential human reality, but only an actual empirical historical reality.

Marx's historical critique showed that the state is not an abstract reality and that it pretends to assume a position above the life of bourgeois society, but actually administers to this life. Marx said that only a primitive political prejudice considers that bourgeois life is necessarily held together by the independent state; in reality, to the contrary, the state is held together by and is a function of bourgeois life.[8] Marx summarized this theory in the "Introduction" to the *Contribution to the Critique of Political Economy* when he said that in his critical work on Hegel's theory of law, he concluded that matters of law and the forms of state can be understood neither in themselves nor through the development of the abstract human spirit. "Legal relations as well as forms of state . . . are rooted in the material conditions of life,"[9] Marx held of the same circumstances analyzed by Hegel and by the French and English philosophers before him in the eighteenth century. Hegel called this framework of economic circumstances the bourgeois or civil society.

Marx's objection to Hegel's theory of the state appears in his explanation of Hegel's theory in the *Critique of Political Economy*. Hegel had incorporated two elements into bourgeois society—legislative enactments and the defense of property as individual possession. Hegel did not regard the functions of property defense as state functions in the strict sense of the concept; rather, he attributed them to bourgeois society itself, having the very character of this society. The defense of property still implies a situation within the realm of utility. Marx wished to show the unreality of Hegel's distinction between the defense of property and the state, whose foundation is law. For as a tool in the hands of bourgeois society, the state is merely the totality of functions protecting bourgeois society and its foundation in private property.

Marx's view can be elucidated with a historical example, a parallelism between Marx's position and Hobbes'. Hobbes explained the emergence of the state as a product of man's renunciation of his freedom in order to guarantee protection from violent death. In the prestate stage, man is in all-out war, and the task of the state is to establish boundaries by exercising its tools of defense.

In his historical-theoretical position, Marx found that the

[8] *MEGA*, I, 3, p. 296.

[9] Karl Marx, *A Contribution to the Critique of Political Economy* (Chicago: C. H. Kerr, 1911), p. 11.

bourgeois society within the state is in an all-inclusive economic struggle, and that the state does not exist as a defensive instrument in this struggle, but as a tool that perpetuates the struggle and provides its lawful sanction. Marx did not intend to explain the historical emergence of the state. He urged a clarification of the essence of the state and its position within human reality. From Marx's viewpoint, the state is not the *result* of the suppression of this total struggle but is rather *held together* by this struggle. Marx's critique of the Hegelian view on the state was based on (1) the rejection of the dichotomy between society and state and (2) the empirical analysis of the state as it is. Two conclusions followed from this reasoning: (*a*) The state was to be eliminated, or as Engels put it, it would wither away. Once the identity between the individual and the whole of society is accomplished, the state becomes superfluous. Freedom, the characteristic feature of a perfectly moral state, becomes the very content of sociey. (*b*) From an empirical standpoint, the present state must be uprooted by revolution, because it perpetuates self-alienation, which also creates egoistic competition and hence gives shape to bourgeois society. Although Hegel understood the state as the realization of the moral idea, Marx maintains that it should cease to be separate from society and become immersed in it. The result is a human society or social humanity; a state that defends bourgeois society, and hence stands in opposition to human society, must be eliminated by the force of critique and by the strength of the real force implied in the critique. The existence of bourgeois society demands a world-change. The idea of self-alienation, discussed in Chapter 7, arises in this, as well as in other matters discussed above.

ELEVENTH THESIS: INTERPRETATION AND CHANGE

> The philosophers have only *interpreted* the world differently; what matters is to *change* it.

The last thesis, the most famous of all even to the point of becoming a watchword, summarizes all the lines of Marx's thought as they were interwoven in the "Theses on Feuerbach." Marx contrasted in this thesis the passive and contemplative attitude toward the world as opposed to the public-social effort to change the world, that is, to change the existing human reality. Marx attempted to juxtapose classical philosophy, especially the philosophy of Hegel, with socialism. The analysis of this attempt shows the contradiction implicit in it, as well as the proximity of the two approaches implicit in the contradiction.

The *"interpretation"* is the philosophical interpretation of the world as it was presented in the suppositions and ideas of Hegel's philosophy. The interpretative and contemplative function of philosophy was formulated by Hegel as follows: "*Hic Rhodus, hic saltus* [Here is Rhodes, here's your jump]. To comprehend what is, this is the task of philosophy, because what is, is reason. Whatever happens, every individual is a child of his time; so philosophy too is its own time apprehended in thoughts. It is just as absurd to fancy that a philosophy can transcend its contemporary world as it is to fancy that an individual can overlap his own age, jump over Rhodes." Hegel goes on to explain his position: "If his theory really goes beyond the world as it is and builds an ideal one as it ought to be, that world exists indeed, but only in his opinions, as an unsubstantial element where anything you please may, in fancy, be built." [10] Hegel also stated in the *Encyklopädie* that, "The purpose of philosophy has always been the intellectual ascertainment [*die denkende Erkenntnis*] of the Idea." [11] The subject matter of philosophy is the ultimate unity or, as Hegel calls it, the absolute unity, which can only be known by way of contemplation, dialectical as it may be, and cannot be practically established by way of deeds and actions. Hegel's theory of the essence of philosophy has two interrelated aspects. Philosophy is a theoretical sphere,

[10] Hegel, *Grundlinien der Philosophie des Rechts,* p. 15; Hegel, *Philosophy of Right,* p. 11.

[11] Hegel, "The Logic of Hegel," *Encyclopaedia of the Philosophical Sciences,* trans. William Wallace (2d edn.; London: Oxford University Press, 1892), p. 354.

a sphere of understanding. This is an aspect from the standpoint of the activity contained within it. However, from the point of view of the subject matter, philosophy is theoretical activity, this being the second aspect, dealing with existing reality, for the real or actual is the rational. Philosophy attempts to understand a perfect and rounded reality within its own limits, without creating a new reality. Life's shape or figure has grown old. The owl of Minerva spreads its wings only with the falling of the dusk.[12] Philosophy deals with rational reality and its function is to raise this reality to its complete consciousness. In other words, rational reality achieves through philosophy complete self-awareness and comprehends itself through reason. The supposition made throughout this view of the essence of philosophy was expressed in Hegel's introduction to his *Philosophy of Right*—the book that Marx criticized and in so doing revealed the principles of his attitude—"What is rational is actual and what is actual is rational." This position on the essence of philosophy was also formulated by Marx in "The Holy Family," with his statement that philosophy is the instrument or tool of the independent consciousness of spirit. The philosopher does not add anything to reality; he appears after it, *"post festum."* [13]

Marx attempted to locate the historical and intellectual position of his new view, the core of which is the new society, defined above as a human society or social humanity as opposed to the present bourgeois society. He wished to emphasize the principle of change as opposed to the principle of contemplation and interpretation. Since the principle of change is stressed, however, the new view necessarily implies an assumption opposed to that of Hegel. Reality is not complete and rational; it is a nonrational reality, in which the idea of man has not yet been realized. Therefore, the reality analyzed by Hegel, the social reality of bourgeois society, is a reality constructed on the antithesis between the individual

[12] Hegel, *Grundlinien der Philosophie des Rechts,* p. 171; Hegel, *Philosophy of Right,* p. 13.

[13] *MEGA,* I, 3, p. 257.

and society, between work and its enjoyment, between society and the state. These antitheses are the empirical proof, as it were, which springs up before our eyes, that reality is not complete, hence not rational. The mark of reason is identity, and the present reality is devoid of identity. Whenever Marx criticized present reality, either in terms of the distinction between society and state, the difference between "bourgeois" and "citoyen," or the difference between what is on earth and in heaven, his point of departure was the rational character of identity. Wherever there is a split, there is a patent antirational factor, which must be overcome in the name of reason and rationality. Henceforth, Marx said that reason always exists, but not always rationally.[14] Reason is not a new historical factor or force that appears only in the new era. Yet the new era is confronted with the critique of reality in the light of reason, a dual critique: a theoretic measurement of reality in the light of the idea and the realization of the idea within reality. The awareness of the antithesis between reason as identity and the divided reality is the basis of the idea of change and is the mark of the new social movement, socialism, the function of which is to realize this identity.

Yet, in this new awareness another matter requires attention. In Marx's opinion, traditional philosophy as contemplation refers to the real as it is, and *by definition* this philosophy does not transcend the actual and thus does not anticipate the future. But what exists is always the given, acquired from the past. Philosophy as contemplation and interpretation is based essentially upon the past, and it knows only two dimensions of time, the past from which the acquisition derives and the present wherein the acquisition is found in actuality. The future is not a dimension of time known to the philosopher contemplatively, whereas the shift from contemplation to change necessarily implies a shift from the past and the present to the future. Marx's contemporary, Sören Kierkegaard, had already said that we understand the past, but we live for the future. The transfer from contemplation to change cor-

[14] Marx, *Der historische Materialismus,* I, p. 225.

responds to the transfer from contemplation to life, from the past to the future. Another contemporary, the Polish philosopher Count August Cieszkowski expressed several of his generation's ideas in salient language.[15] He argued against the historical position of Hegel on the basis that it reduced the dimensions of time, for it knew merely the past and the present, not the future. The future is not bound to given and formulated facts (*Tatsachen*); it is sustained by the deeds (*Taten*) of men that implement goals. Hence, Cieszkowski regarded the new historical period as marked by deeds, whereas previous historical periods had been marked by facts.

The transfer from interpretation to change follows from the revelation of the wide gap between reason and existing reality. This transfer qua change bridges the gap by the realization of reason within reality or by the elevation of reality to the level of reason.

This brings us to Marx's opinion, which can be understood in the following way. The relation between the theoretical interpretation of the world and change is not merely an antithetical relation, for change also bridges the wide gap between the content contrived by contemplation, showing identity, the mark of reason, and reality that has not as yet reached the level of reason. Change and the socialism based on it carry us toward the future. Change realizes reason, or as Marx succinctly put it, realizes philosophy. Philosophy as the sphere of theory must necessarily cease to be a theoretical sphere and become a real one; in this change, it will cease to appear in the world in its narrow confines. However, in exchange, it will acquire the "flesh and sinew" of a living and active reality. Philosophy will gain in reality what it renounced in isolating the theoretical sphere.[16]

How is the transition made from philosophy to reality?

[15] Count August Cieszkowski, *Prolegomena zur Historiosophie* (2d edn.; Posen: J. Leitgeberg Co., 1908; originally published in 1838), pp. 16 ff.

[16] Marx, Doctoral Dissertation, *Der historische Materialismus,* I, p. 17.

Questions about the theoretical domain are common to Marx and the young Hegelian generation, both those counted among the socialist thinkers, such as Moses Hess, or those on the threshold of socialism, such as August Cieszkowski. However, there is a division of opinion concerning the force that ejected reason from its theoretical domain. This matter may be clarified by the discussion of three types of thought; the third is Marx's theory.

"Philosopher's Stone." Count August Cieszkowski said that perfect rational knowledge is like the "philosopher's stone" after which the alchemists in the Middle Ages searched. They wanted to discover this philosopher's stone not for its own sake but in order to smelt it and produce gold ore. If likened to the stone of wisdom, rational knowledge must of necessity be a tool in the hands of the deed. True philosophy is the philosophy of the act. August Cieszkowski uses the term *"Praxis,"* that is, the inference of real conclusions by means of reason. Rational philosophy, therefore, is the instrument of the act, it does not blaze its own path to reality. Reality is dependent, as it were, upon philosophy, which serves as a pathfinder.

The Moral Goal. The second view is related to the analysis of Georg Lukács, who wished to distinguish between Marx, on the one hand, and Moses Hess and Ferdinand Lassalle on the other. The details of Lukács debate with Hess and Lassalle need not be discussed, but a discussion of Lukács' analysis provides a typology of the various theories. The second view started with the idea of the active essence of Spirit, the same essence at which Marx hints in the first thesis and which was analyzed in the first excursus. If the nature of Spirit is in activity, it is once again impossible for it to reach satiation within the limits of theory, which is characteristic of philosophy. The active Spirit continues to carry out its life in action. The step beyond philosophy is entrance into reality and the formation of reality according to the philosophical imperative. Lukács argued that when Hess and Lassalle spoke about the activity of Spirit they did not conceive it as operating according to its own laws. They linked the activity of Spirit to the attempt to materialize the ideal moral goal. Therefore, Hess and Lassalle transferred theory from given reality to the moral goal fixed as an imperative or as an "ought" opposite reality. They did not place the active factor in reality, and it did not move by a dialectical force inherent in it, but by the force of the ideal moral goal beyond reality. Lukács formulated this idea by saying that Hess and Lassalle transcended the contemplation of the Hegelian school and the philosophy based on the given, not by means of a complete exhaustion of the significance of Hegel's dialectical motives, but by recourse to Fichte's idea of the moral goal. Because the moral goal is beyond the given reality, a deed that draws given reality nearer to the distant moral ideal is needed. This view deviates from the factor of interpretation and calls for change, not by the force of the immanent given character of reality, but by the force gained by transcending this reality. It has ceased to be a theory of the dialectic and has become an abstract moral aspiration. In this perspective, the criticism that Hegel leveled against all attempts to transcend reality to create an imaginary "should-be" moral world is applicable. This clarification serves as a *typological* presentation, not as a precise explanation of the theory of Hess.

Reality Changing Itself. The main representative of the third theory was Marx, who attempted to reveal the force sponsoring the new reality within given reality itself. The view is dialectical in that it regards reality as given within the rhythm of dynamic tension. The dynamic is not imposed from without by the proximating force of this reality directed toward approach to the absolute idea fixed beyond it. However, the new reality is defined and has a specific content; it is the reality of human society. In human society the human world is brought back to man himself, thus bringing about the identity between man and the circumstances of his life.[17] Yet identity qua dialectical comprehensiveness is the main category of philosophy in the speculative sense. The pressing problem is: Where within the given dichotomy of social reality is the vantage point for human society, or, where does philosophy enter the divided reality? The answer as it appears in Marx's writings has many aspects, but its essentials can be elucidated as follows.

What original supposition did Marx make? It was the Hegelian supposition of the power of reason. Reason is not a passive capacity; it is reality. Marx put the emphasis on the first part of the famous Hegelian dictum: "What is rational is actual." Marx argued against Hegel's philosophy of right that it did not deal critically with presuppositions of philosophy itself and that the only way to preserve philosophy was to negate prior philosophy. Thus, Marx continued, the way to realize philosophy is to remove it from its own abstract, speculative confinement. Philosophy as a speculative development of reason lets reason remain partial only, because as abstract, it is partial. The notion of the comprehensiveness of reason leads reason toward realization in the world.[18] Within reason itself is found the force that extricates it from theory and transforms it into actual reality. The contradiction suggested by Marx between reason and its nonrational forms of existence is reconciled by the force of reason itself. Engels formulated this idea in saying that all prior philosophy was obligated to understand the world as rational. What is rational is also necessary, and what is necessary must be real or become real. This is the bridge to the great practical acts of the new philosophy. What is the nature of the bridge?

Practical Energy. The first line of thought in this inquiry was formulated in the language of psychology. Marx argued that

[17] Marx, *Der historische Materialismus,* I, p. 255.
[18] Marx, *Der historische Materialismus,* I, p. 271.

a psychological law is present in the fact that a theoretical spirit that has been freed eventually becomes a practical energy, a will that turns against the reality circumscribing it.[19] Marx wanted to express the idea that subjective identification with a certain truth or with a certain theoretical viewpoint simultaneously removes the theory from its confined realm and makes it a force of will. This sounds like Socrates' idea about the activating power of correct understanding.

Masses. This psychological explanation does not suffice, however, for it is not yet determined who possesses the theoretical knowledge, the identification that motivates a person to acts and actions that originate in will. The second line of Marx's thought on this matter is related to a precise definition of the will, involving the determination of the sphere wherein the transition from theory to the power of active will takes place. The weapon of criticism is not in any way made to take the place of the critique of the weapon. Material force must necessarily be transformed by material force, but theory also becomes a material force when it penetrates into the masses.[20] Because of their practical needs and interest in emancipation, the masses—pointing to the proletariat as the subject of the deed that transforms—are the meeting ground between theory and the practice nurtured from it. Here is the bridge between rational knowledge and the historical deed. Philosophy finds its material weapon in the proletariat, while the proletariat finds in philosophy its spiritual weapon.[21]

Needs. What is the nature of this meeting, and what is the real historical subject in which it occurs? This is not a confrontation between lucid reason and an opaque mass; it is a meeting between reason and the needs of the masses, as a motive force for action and historical change. And so Marx

[19] Marx, *Der historische Materialismus,* p. 16.
[20] Marx, *Der historische Materialismus,* p. 272.
[21] Marx, *Der historische Materialismus,* p. 279.

said that theory realizes itself within society only to the extent to which it is a realization of society's needs.[22] Marx distinguished here between theory and its realization, which does not correspond to an abstract theoretical rhythm but to the historical reality of the real needs of society. The movement from abstract theory to the real act is not merely a psychological process; Marx was dealing with the active forces of society, the most fundamental of which are its needs. The concept of need appears to hold a central position in Marx's theory; this very concept was met in the elucidation of the concept of practice. Practice is the creator of our demands and it creates the means for their supply. The central Marxian concept of practice is also the bridge between theory in its narrow sense and reality, insofar as this concept by its nature has two aspects, for it is a dialectical concept. It is the source of reality, and it needs and it gives direction to the course of reality. It is then related to theory, which is the medium disclosing the structure of reality and its meaning.

Proletariat. The concept "need" is not an abstract concept. In historical-sociological reality it appears embodied in a specific social class. Need is the decisive distinguishing mark of the proletariat. The proletariat is the very stratum within human reality as such that does not have a place within this reality. The existing human reality is a reality of the bourgeois society. The proletariat is placed within bourgeois society in that it sells its labor as merchandise. Yet it has no place in bourgeois society, for it has no property. Property and its defense are the constituent characteristics of bourgeois society. The place of the proletariat within bourgeois society is therefore dialectical. It is dependent on this society, but it is not placed within it as such. In the proletariat are concentrated, as in a historical-empirical concentrate, all the flaws of bourgeois society. This concentration and concurrently the interest in human emancipation make it possible for the

[22] Marx, *Der historische Materialismus,* pp. 273–274; *see also* "Excursus: Rousseau and Marx," in Chapter 3.

proletariat to be the subject and bearer of social change and eventually the creator of social humanity. These points identify the human position of the proletariat as the subject of the realization of philosophy, philosophy being understood as the conception of the identity of the world in general and of the unity of human history in particular. All the evils and crimes of present society are concentrated in the single proletariat class. Therefore the revolution of society and the existence of the proletariat as a specific social class in bourgeois society necessarily correspond. The needs of the proletariat lead it toward a vital interest in the establishment of a human society that will represent the universal self-liberation of mankind. An identity exists, therefore, between the interests of the proletariat and the goals of human society as a whole. Philosophy cannot realize itself without the elevation of the proletariat, and the proletariat cannot elevate itself without the realization of philosophy.[23]

The proletariat will find its place within human reality, when that reality ceases to be constructed on property and when property ceases to dominate men who create it. In its place will be a reality based on the identity of man with the conditions of his life. Marx was not satisfied with the psychological proximity between theory and action. In keeping with his principal assumptions, he urged the proximity between theory and historical reality, which is always a specific entity formed by specific forces operating within it. Therefore, Marx related the theory of identity to the reality of human needs and the concrete-historical subject of present needs, the proletariat. This class outside of society is the actual proof that society is not built upon identity, and this class is the subject of the new society.[24]

By discovering the proximity between reason and need, or between philosophy and the proletariat, Marx seemed to have freed himself from the difficulty pointed out by Hegel in, "Here is Rhodes, here's your jump." We no longer have an

[23] Marx, *Der historische Materialismus,* pp. 276, 280.
[24] Marx, *Der historische Materialismus,* p. 279.

imaginary transcending of given reality or a programmatic blueprint for a new society built upon a vision or upon the imperative implied in the "ought." Marx held to the given reality and its immanent aims. He aligned himself with Hegel's phrase, but the "here" was interpreted in its widest sense; that is, Marx no longer saw only the "here," the bourgeois society, as identical with the existing society. He saw the "here" at many levels, containing within it the force of history and the subject of the history of the new order. He interpreted the leap precisely. He regarded the "here" not as a relaxed, self-contained reality but as a reality within which lay the core of the new reality, indicating the direction of the leap from the existing to the new reality.

With this background, the relation between philosophy and the proletariat is established, the relation between the understanding of the world and the change taking place within it. The proletariat achieves the status of the subject of philosophy and philosophy becomes the spiritual weapon of the proletariat. The head of this emancipation is philosophy, Marx said, its *heart* is the *proletariat*.[25] Philosophy finds within the proletariat its material weapons, and the proletariat finds within philosophy its spiritual weapons. The elimination of philosophy to which Marx referred meant a close inner-mutuality between philosophy and the proletariat. Marx did not become disillusioned with philosophy. The elimination of philosophy, as he referred to it from time to time, did not reflect recalcitrance or nihilism. He did not substitute another theory or another system of ideas and experiences for it, as did Kierkegaard, who left philosophy because of disappointment and turned to faith. Marx eliminated philosophy because he took it seriously; he called for life impregnated with philosophy, with the realization of the dialectical identity that is the content of philosophy as a speculative development of reason. Philosophy does not compel a way of life and emotional reactions, as did the attitude of the Stoics or Spinoza. Philosophy does not imply an individualistic idea of a wise

[25] Marx, *Der historische Materialismus,* p. 280.

man with an image and a character inherent in his viewpoint. Philosophy implies a human reality, a social reality at that. Perhaps here Marx approached Plato's philosophical attitude more than any other, in so closely relating a synoptic philosophical outlook with a view on the nature of the state or of society. However, as Hegel already had astutely commented in the introduction to his *Philosophy of Right,* Plato related philosophy to the inner meaning of the existing Greek reality, whereas Marx connected philosophy with the human reality that has not yet come into existence. Therefore, the philosophical ideal of Plato was perceived as an ideal of contemplation which comes after action, while the Marxian ideal of philosophy was one of content-filled activity, the realization of the rational content. Philosophy could not be eliminated without its materialization.[26] Socialism was conceived, as Engels commented, as the inheritor of philosophy.

The main lines of Marx's thought can now be traced, as they arise out of the "Theses on Feuerbach." Marx opened his inquiry with the clarification of the concept of practice, which is the fundamental or arch-concept in all his ideas. Practice eliminates the dichotomy between man and his life-circumstances; it realizes the identity that is the mark of human society. Also practice removes the dichotomy between theory and action. It bridges philosophy and the building and altering effort of man. The sphere of practice is society. Society is the subject of change as well as its object, for it changes itself. However, the concrete society, to which we refer, is bourgeois society; it modifies itself when the modification is sustained by the proletariat, which has no position within this society. This change ushers in the consolidation of the new society, the human society or social humanity. The consolidation of the new society contains all the elements referred to as constituting the essence of practice. It is the society of the identity between man and the circumstances of his life, of the realization of theory in practice, and of emancipated practice

[26] Marx, *Der historische Materialismus,* p. 280.

saturated with rational content. It is evident that this means the identity of society with practice, for only then is it possible to argue that the practical world is an act of reason, be the act what it may be.[27]

The danger of inferring such a conclusion from Marx's theory is evident from his theory. Even Marx himself did not intend to identify every action as an alleged act of the realization of philosophy. Marxism, principally Bolshevism, as it developed is related to this perverted idea of the realization of philosophy, identifying the deeds of a regime as the necessary realization of an idea.

[27] The literature on Marx's philosophy is growing and in academic philosophy a new wave of interest in his doctrine is apparent. It would be impossible to list all the relevant books, but a few can be mentioned, in addition to those already referred to in the text, from which I have greatly profited:

H. B. Acton, *The Illusion of the Epoch: Marxism-Leninism as a Philosophical Creed* (London: Cohent West, 1955).

Karl Barth, *Wahrheit und Ideologie* (Zurich: Manesse, 1945).

August Cornu, *Karl Marx: l'homme et l'oeuvre* (Paris: Felix Alcan, 1934).

G. Lichtheim, *Marxism: An Historical and Critical Study* (London: Routledge and Kegan, 1961).

Karl Löwith, *Von Hegel bis Nietzsche* (Zurich and New York: Europa, 1941).

Georg Lukács, *Geschichte und Klassenbewusstsein: Studien über Marxistische Dialektik* (Berlin: Malik, 1923).

Robert C. Tucker, *Philosophy and Myth in Karl Marx* (Cambridge, England: The Cambridge University Press, 1961).

CHAPTER 6

Poverty of Philosophical Speculation

REALIZATION OR EXPROPRIATION?

The commentary on the "Theses on Feuerbach" closed with the analysis of the way in which philosophy comes to fruition. The very fact that philosophy has to be realized implies that it is intrinsically rich, but also attests to its necessary poverty. Marx discusses this poverty of philosophy in his book against Pierre Proudhon.

Marx's book, *The Poverty of Philosophy,*[1] is without a doubt one of his most poignant works. It is important for the formulation of his own ideas, for the polemic carried on with his colleagues, and particularly for the determination of his own relation to philosophy. The title Marx gave to this book was derived from the title of a book by Proudhon, *The Philosophy of Poverty.*[2] Nevertheless, Marx had some justification for using this title even though it approximated Proudhon's; beyond Marx's great love for acid language and for alliteration, it was his intention to show the poverty in the very nature of philosophical inquiry, as an inquiry involving con-

[1] Karl Marx, *The Poverty of Philosophy: Being a Translation of* La Misère de la Philosophie (*A Reply to* La Philosophie de la Misère *of M. Proudhon*), trans. Harry Quelch (Chicago: C. H. Kerr, 1916). All references in this chapter to this title are from the Quelch translation.

[2] Proudhon's full title was *Système des Contradictions économiques; ou, Philosophie de la Misère* (Paris: Guillaumin, 1846).

templation and abstraction, and the poverty in the conclusions of the inquiry whenever they touch on the actual reality of man and his future. He found it necessary, therefore, to substitute for this inquiry something that would progress beyond philosophy and bring it to its realization, that is, an economic-intellectual inquiry arising in a Marxian theory to become the inheritor of a comprehensive philosophical world view.

Personal Polemic. Marx's acidity in the polemic against Proudhon is of a relevant conceptual character. In addition, the polemic reveals a personal negative evaluation. As is well known, Marx was not an easy friend and a difficult adversary. He took advantage of the evident weaknesses of Proudhon, such as his ignorance of German, which he himself admits, and his lack of direct access to philosophical writings, especially those of Hegel, even though he felt himself influenced by these works. Marx argued that Proudhon used Hegelian-type phrases (pages 114–115) and did not in point of fact understand the method of the dialectic. In his typical mocking sarcasm, Marx said, "Let us for an instant take M. Proudhon himself as a category" (page 122) and goes on to indicate that Proudhon did not use the dialectical manner. "It is not the category which poses and opposes itself by its contradictory nature; it is M. Proudhon who disturbs himself, argues with himself, and strives and struggles between the two sides of the category." It is evident that Marx is engaging in a bitter personal criticism, when he says that the disturbance is to be attributed to the author and not to the content in front of him. Perhaps the rather haughty personal attack of the argument reaches its peak in Marx's statement that Proudhon is only of the petty bourgeoisie, tossed about constantly between capital and labor, political economy and communism (page 137).

No doubt to a certain extent Marx was not fair to Proudhon, not because Marx argued against his philosophical importance, but because he argued against Proudhon's personal vacillation. Marx and Proudhon's letter of 1846 in which he testified to his own condition as antidogmatic and said that he preferred to burn property in a small fire rather than spread new flames by a Bartholomean night turned against the owners of property. If Proudhon's weakness lay in deficient intellectual capacity, then Marx's criticism of Proudhon is a kind of exposure by the powerful of the weak. The weakness of Proudhon was the product of a conscious attitude, which showed awareness of the boundaries of dogmatism and led to arguments in the name of skepticism. In the violent polemic, Marx did not refer respectfully to the fully admitted conscious assumptions and limitations deriving from the attitude of his opponent. Marx himself did not prefer to burn his opponents in small fires.

Yet the main results of the analysis presented here are the philosophical assumptions of Marx's theory and the extent to which the polemic with Proudhon reveals these assumptions. A scholar of our own age, a critical admirer of Marx, offers evidence of the proximity of Marx and Proudhon, especially on matters of economic theory. J. A. Schumpeter admits that Proudhon cannot be regarded as an important economic thinker and that his books are full of distorted observations and serious logical errors. Schumpeter thought, however, that Proudhon influenced Marx on such important economic issues as the productivity of capital and land.[3] Schumpeter shows that the historical account is not closed; however, we are not concerned at present with this account.

Abstractness. In his letter, Proudhon called Marx a philosopher and undoubtedly this name was in accord with the conceptual usage of the time. Marx in his book against Proudhon called him the "true philosopher" (page 119). In this book, the fundamental position of Marx against philosophy as an engagement in abstractions becomes markedly clear. Hence, we must discuss the various terms and implications contained

[3] Joseph Schumpeter, *Economic Doctrine and Method: An Historical Sketch,* trans. R. Aris (London: Allen & Unwin, 1954), p. 122.

in Marx's argument. It is interesting to note that Marx did not direct his attack against abstraction as a general philosophical position. He objected to abstract inquiries into the matter of human reality in general and into matters of economic reality in particular. And he said, "What Hegel has done for religion, right, etc., M. Proudhon seeks to do for political economy" (page 116).

What is this abstract occupation with matters of political economics? We shall investigate one example (page 84). Proudhon and others discussed economic exchange as personal exchange between two individuals, abstracting from the framework of society and history in which these exchanges take place. Marx pointed out two distinguishing characteristics of such abstract discussion. (1) This discussion isolates the individual man from his social surroundings and transforms him into an atomic creature. Abstraction means here the isolation of individuals from the social whole. (2) Abstraction takes place when the processes as they occur in actuality are not followed and when the creation of an artificial model, or the fabrication of processes in preferred; the argument being that this fabrication reflects or describes reality as it is. Marx wrote that, "He pushes abstraction to the farthest limits, in confounding all producers in a single producer, all consumers in a single consumer, and in establishing the struggle between these two chimerical personages. But in the real world matters go otherwise. The competition between those who offer and the competition between those who demand forms a necessary element in the struggle between buyers and sellers" (page 45). The detachment of the individual from society and the concern with an imaginary model of society cause deviations from the dynamic nature of social reality. Marx's argument against the abstraction of Proudhon's inquiry, resulting from its philosophical nature, is also the substance of the Marxian argument against the socialist utopia. Utopia in general, and the socialist utopia in particular, are kinds of imaginary models. They represent the result and the manifestation of isolation from existing reality and the creation of another pattern of reality in its stead. Abstraction, therefore, is present in the foundation of utopia itself. Marx's argument against the abstract character of the economic analysis of Proudhon is thus but a detail of his arguments against abstraction in general, as in the first thesis on Feuerbach.

It can be urged that Marx exaggerated to such an extent in his arguments against abstraction that he began to become hyperbolic and that, at any rate, his conclusions are refutable. For example: "In each historical epoch property is differently developed, and in a series of social relations entirely different. Thus, to define bourgeois property is nothing other than to explain all the social relations of bourgeois production. To pretend to give a definition of property as of an independent relation, a separate category, an abstract and eternal idea, can only be an illusion of metaphysics or of jurisprudence" (page 168). Initially, Marx said that property developed in different historical periods and its nature was determined by the nature of the social relations. Therefore, the nature of a specific property in a specific historical period, such as bourgeois property, cannot be defined without referring to the period. It follows that the definition of a specific property is nothing but the description of the social and economic conditions of this particular society. Later, however, Marx exaggerated even more, saying that property cannot be defined at all without referring to a historical period. Marx did not want to deny that property exists in social reality. But does the *concept* "property" have no meaning at all? If it had no general reference, how could Marx use the concept property in referring to both the feudal and the capitalist periods? Does Marx want to assert that the use of the concept "property" is merely nominalistic? It would be difficult to hold that Marx was a nominalist in this matter. It is evident that there are constant factors in all property, independent of the actual historical scene, such as ownership and the actual legal sanction to use whatever the property owner has in his possession. Marx's emphasis on reality and history, dealt with later, caused him to exaggerate here. It appears not only in his nominalistic tone in whatever concerns concepts in general, but in his treatment of the constant factors in the historical evolution of property. In summary, the argument against abstraction is cogent in its proper place, that is, it is adequate against the substitution of a model for reality. The development of natural science in our time testifies to this. But the argument against abstraction does not apply to what is presented as essentially abstract, that is, to the concept; and the concept of property clearly is a *concept.* The argument does not apply to the relations existing in a complex reality, such as the relation of ownership, and the authority to exhibit ownership. This relation is not abstract, for it is a part of actual reality. Marx substituted the argument against the abstract for an argument against the constancy of features in a phenomenon like property, and these two are not one and the same thing. The serious effects of this substitution will be apparent in the discussion of the nature of man.

Man and Function. What led Marx to argue against Proudhon that, "We have now to talk metaphysics while speaking of political economy" (page 112)? The debate with Proudhon on the question of the "established value" sheds light on this central topic. Marx understood Proudhon's treatment, and it seems that he understood it correctly, as the attempt to determine the absolute value of goods, a value independent of the circumstances in which the product is produced, in which it reaches exchange, and in which it is used by the consumer. To translate Marx's view into this language, it seems that he thought that Proudhon, as it were, sought to determine the *natural law,* as a law implied in the nature of reality, and thus hidden behind the *positive law,* connoting the law regulating the human conditions and social life here and now implemented by legal and political authorities governing and enforcing law. Proudhon thereby offered a solution to the socio-economic question whether the "established value" as the natural law should be the economic norm. Or, again, that the actual positive law should dominate society. The detachment of the value of merchandise from the actual historical-social circumstances is merely an abstraction. Here Marx's statement is correct. This abstraction is not proper, since what is referred to is not the abstraction of concept or the detachment of the stable factor from surrounding circumstances. That to which reference is made is isolation of something that must not be isolated, that is, the actual value of merchandise or products. Marx was inclined to call all isolation of this kind "mystification." However, it seems that he was right when he argued that there is a kind of mystification in assuming the possibility of an established value. A mystification results if the attempt is made to discover a fundamental value separate from the merchandise. In opposition to this abstraction, Marx urges a return to reality. One of the distinguishing marks of this reality is that neither the producer nor the consumer have a free choice (page 44), and that a free buyer and a free producer are nonexistent when abstracted from circumstances, for they are actual and concrete agents. Since there is no absolute or established value beyond the economic circumstances, money is no longer viewed as a thing but as a social relation (page 86). The result of these considerations and analyses is not merely a new emphasis on actual reality in contradistinction to a model, but a further element is involved. When reality is approached abstractly, the relations between men (human relations as distinct from intermerging economic relations) cease to exist. On the abstract level, there are no concrete economic relations, only essences and categories. Furthermore, economic relations become decisive within concrete reality: "These relations are not the relations of individual to individual, but of workman to capitalist, of farmer to landlord, etc." (page 109). Reality is not merely the antithesis of abstraction. It is a plane whose unique character is in the economic relations dominating it and enveloping the remainder of the relations in its plane. "And what is it that he has effectively proved? That commerce is more sovereign than the monarch. Let the monarch order that a mark shall henceforth be two marks, commerce will always tell you that these two marks are only worth one mark as before" (page 93). In abstraction, that is, in the detachment of the model, Proudhon acted freely toward reality; he saw himself free to determine the relations according to normative measures. There was a need in his system, therefore, for the concept of the "established value," a value not determined by the circumstances but by reason and the economic and legal fictions. But in dealing with reality, according to Marx, the regular and determined course of events must be acknowleged in terms of reality itself and not in terms of a distinct exterior norm. Marx did not examine at this point the concept of alienation, the idea that within economic reality the sovereignty of man is expropriated, and man is subordinated to the products he himself creates. However, there is no doubt that this idea is in the background in these analyses elucidating the valid authority of reality in its actual relationships.

Has Marx shown that the power of reality reaches a point where all the relations existing within it become one and are no longer human relations but mere functional relations? Are they no longer relations between one individual and another, but only between workman and capitalist, for instance? Behind Marx's extreme analysis stands the concept of a comprehensive self-alienation within social reality. In order to gain the full import of the idea of this comprehensive and singular alienation of man from himself, it must first be determined that: (1) The power is inherent in all social relations to expropriate man completely from his essence and thus reduce him to an agent who only fulfills a function within social circumstances. (2) Man has no essence that can remain separate from and not eradicated by economic reality. Although in this particular book, Marx himself is inclined to the most extreme view that man has no constant essence, it is precisely this idea that is difficult to maintain or support from Marx's own analysis. For if man did not have an essence, the essence of a free creature not enslaved to its products, there would be no place for even a conceptual distinction between man as an individual and man as a self fulfilling an economic function, as is a workman or capitalist. Even though Marx was extreme in his formulations, we must adopt the idea that he assumed that man has a nature, even though it has become muddled and confused within economic reality. The more Marx attempted to clarify the power of reality factually, the more he tended to show the perversions that man undergoes in terms of his metaphysical essence ceasing to be man and becoming only an industrialist or worker. Thus Marx evaluated reality from the point of view of man's comprehensive nature, which became restricted and dismembered in the prevailing social conditions. To put it differently, Marx had no refuge from metaphysics when he criticized reality as having power over its own course of events, even though this reality is nothing but a perverted system when viewed in terms of the essential nature of man.

If the distinction between man as an individual and man in terms of an economic function is accepted, the question can be asked: Is a complete obfuscation of the human essence possible? Is it conceivable that man becomes merely an agent of an economic function? It seems that in the excitement of the polemic against utopian abstraction, Marx became caught up in what may be called *deterministic abstraction,* which caused him to attribute the decisive force of man to economic reality. It would have been enough if Marx had simply said that there is a contradiction between human relations and economic relations; or that there is a predominance of economic relations over human relations; for then he would not have been forced to such a radical statement as that human relations are completely nonexistent. He could have shown that economic relations are not human relations, and hence he would not have reached a level of abstraction at which he claimed that reality is nothing but economic relations. In summary, since the idea of the overwhelming force of economic relations could not stand on its own logic, Marx was led to the assumption or conclusion that economic relations are the comprehensive relations in human reality. When Marx said, "The right is only the official recognition of the fact" (page

94) he wanted to make this include the economic right; but again, the argument of universality does not hold. It can be agreed that an economic right is the formulation of an economic fact, just as a physical law is the formulation of a fact, that is, the reality of nature. But when Marx broadened the formulation, saying, "The same men who establish social relations conformable with their material productivity, produce also the principle, the ideas, the category, conformable with their social relations" (page 119), this was a broad formulation that included a great deal more than was necessary. It involved him in serious difficulties. What are the types of principles, ideas, and categories about which he spoke? If he was talking about economic principles, there is no quarrel. However, Marx did not formulate the matter solely on the basis of the relation between economic principles and the economic domain, but as a general statement based upon the use of the concept *category*. Is the category of reality, for example, determined by the realm of social relations? Marx referred to those individuals who establish economic relations and categories, as the same. Did he hold that, since the real man is the determined agent of economic relations, he is also the one who thinks up the categories of reality? This touches on the inner limitations of the philosophy of Marx. Precisely because he wanted to show the dependence of human reality on man, he was inclined to make an exaggerated interpretation of human reality. He placed in it everything that exists within the horizon of man, including principles and categories. Yet what is found within man's horizon is not as such the product of man *in* his social relations. That man lives in a changing reality does not transform all contents in this reality into a passing historical product. The Marxian attachment to actual social reality leads rather to radical historicist conclusions containing no internal necessity with respect to the issue under discussion, even if it is agreed with Marx that reality has a power of its own.[4] Even assuming with Marx that

[4] *See* Nathan Rotenstreich, *Spirit and Man* (The Hague: Martinus Nijhoff, 1963).

work is a process occurring between man and nature and that man establishes his own metabolism with nature through his own act, it would not follow that there is no structure of physical nature that has to be comprehended and understood as such. Man's act may be related to changing historical conditions, but the structure of nature, thus in a way absorbed in history through the historical act, does not cease to have its own character, which has to be taken into consideration by human beings in their historical acts. Man changes nature, although within the limits of the structure of nature. It seems that Marx's radical historicism as exhibited here—even for the sake of polemic objectives—blurs the distinction between changing acts in nature, and nature as a structure of its own.

Another way to formulate the position of social reality is to emphasize the historicity of this reality, rather than the statements and the abstractions of Proudhon's theory. The subsequent discussion of the meaning of the Marxian concept of history shows that it is not at all univocal. One of the weak points of the entire system is that it uses the concept of history in its broad and hence ambiguous sense. (1) Marx stressed that, according to Proudhon (page 125), there is no room for *becoming,* because things did not come to be. Such factors as economic-social relations and economic laws are given a priori, according to Proudhon. Since there is no becoming, there is no dissolution. (2) Therefore, Marx felt entitled to identify history with flux (page 119). But this conclusion is not at all necessary. Even if it is believed that relations come about and are not given from the very beginning, it is not necessary to hold that these relations are in flux. At any rate, it is not implied that all that comes into being passes away again. In this matter, Marx seemed to accept as obvious certain cosmological assumptions, particularly those of the Middle Ages: since the world was created, it necessarily ends in time, it is transient. But Marx should have clarified the relation between what is coming to be and what is transitory and fleeting, as well as one other decisive matter—that knowledge may also come into being and pass away, so that there was a time when this or that phenomena was not known as it is known now. Did Marx want to say that what is known is in flux, for it was arrived at *through* an evolving process? It can be conjectured, for instance, that the idea of human rights came about in specific circumstances. First it was nonexistent, or was not considered valid, but now it is thought valid. Does the fact of the evolution of knowledge also imply the fact of the passing away of the content of what is known until it is no longer valid in any circumstance? In this decisive matter, Marx did not distinguish between coming to be and validity, and this failure is representative of his system in general. (3) Therefore, Marx opposed the position that the principle determines history and instead maintained the idea that history determines the principle. But, again, the meaning of this statement must be queried. Is the meaning simply neutral, namely, that any principle arises in specific historical circumstances, as does the principle of individualism, which, according to Marx, arose in specific circumstances? On the other hand, how does history as a process give rise to principles? Whence do principles come? Are not facts and events alone sufficient for history, without the formulation of principles at all? Is the very *realm* of principles determined by history? By not arguing through or clarifying the distinction between coming to be and validity, Marx failed to explain the relation between the spheres of principles and contents. He subsequently assumed in his famous statement, "Existence determines consciousness," the unilateral dependence of principles upon history. This issue is discussed subsequently in this chapter.

(4) One of the renowned statements in Marx's writings is: "Labor is organized and divided, variously, according to the instruments which it manipulates. The wind-mill supposes a division of labor quite other than that of the steam mill. To begin by the division of labor in general in order to arrive at a specific instrument of production, machinery, is therefore to fly in the face of history" (page 145). But it is difficult to find out what exactly Marx meant. Was he saying that di-

vision of labor is inseparable from historical (economic and social) *circumstances* and depends on them and changes with them, or was he saying that division of labor is by *nature* nothing but a historical phenomenon, that is, that a human reality without a division of labor can be imagined as a matter of principle? It seems that Marx was inclined to a complete historical interpretation of the phenomenon of division of labor. He asked that it be viewed as a mere historical phenomenon, since according to his theory division of labor is a phenomenon that evolved in changing historical circumstances and, therefore, can be transformed by other circumstances. But it is not necessary to view the matter in this way. At any rate, from an empirical-historical standpoint this is a serious matter, for the division of labor is to be found in one form or another in every known society. Marx himself realized its ultimate root in the differences between man and woman. The division of labor is revealed in the past in different historical forms and circumstances. Nevertheless, it is not merely a historical matter. It seems that Marx was forced to this position by an optimistic view that came to him through observation or through a historicist interpretation. Doubtlessly, Marx regarded division of labor in bourgeois society as the sign of distress of society and humanity and the root of all evil. From a certain perspective, the division into social classes is a distorting and oppressive manifestation of the division of labor. Since Marx urged a total elimination of human social distress, he identified the division of labor creating the proletariat with social evil and held that by social (historical) methods it is possible to eliminate the evil completely. His reliance on history and his emphasis on its importance did not keep him from taking the decisive leap beyond history at this point. Here a very exaggerated utopian vision is encountered, expressed in a total *attachment* to history, as Marx understood it. The division of labor manifests the moral pathos of Marx and this pathos can be said to refer to the "evangelist" in Marx.

In several central sections of his book, Marx played the role of both philosopher and evangelist. "In short," he assented, "by the introduction of machinery, the division of labor within society has been developed, the task of the workman within the factory has been simplified, capital has been accumulated, and man has been further dismembered" (page 153). Several aspects of this statement are important: (1) It is clear that the moral emphasis, the emphasis on analysis, has been placed at the end of the sentence, at which Marx referred to the *dismembering* of man; (2) Marx clearly held that there is "a more or less" in the division of labor, and therefore he analyzed social reality according to "more or less"; (3) Marx spoke about *man* and not only about workman or capitalist. He used concepts here that imply a theory maintaining the existence of a constant and permanent human essence.

Other examples of a moral pathos appear in the historical and sociological analyses of Marx: "Certainly the language of Ricardo is almost cynical. To put in the same category the cost of manufacturing hats and the cost of subsistence of man, is to transform man into a hat. The cynicism is in the things themselves, and not in the words which express these things" (page 54). This statement is again characteristic of a moral pathos struggling against the degradation of man and against placing his subsistence on a level with hats. It reveals the authentic pathos of Marx, a man who wanted to "see things as they are" and to call them by their proper names. This led him to the point where he was not afraid to call man by the name of merchandise when reality was such that man was merchandise. Another very pregnant expression of the same pathos is to be found in Marx's unconscious equivocation in using the word "poverty": (1) in the sense of the establishment of an economic fact and (2) in the sense of a moral and perhaps aesthetic analysis. "Why, then, are cotton, potatoes and spirit the pivots of bourgeois society? . . . Because in a society based upon poverty, the poorest products have the fatal prerogative of serving the use of the greatest number" (page 67). Products are poor not because they are the cheapest, but because they are the products of which the impoverished are in need, since their food value and social value is low and even inferior. This statement is also characteristic of Marx's ability to be overflexible in the use of caustic linguistic combinations and formulas.

Harmony. In the description of the dialectic and its essence it is often said that its basis lies in the view that there is no "either . . . or" but "this as well as that." The debate between Marx and Proudhon suggests that such a summary of the dialectical position is far from satisfactory, for it hardly corresponds to the matter itself. Marx argued against Proudhon, apparently with justification, that the latter wanted to maintain the good side of economic phenomena, such as division of labor, through the elimination of the evils occurring in the application (page 121). At one point Marx said with increased acrimoniousness: "He takes the first category to hand and arbitrarily attributes to it the quality of becoming a remedy to the inconvenience of the category which he wishes to purify. Thus imposts, if we are to believe M. Proudhon, remedy the inconveniences of imposts; landlordism, the inconveniences of credit" (page 123). In order to comprehend what Marx meant by this, we are led to say that he thought that Proudhon viewed a variety of economic phenomena as self-repairing mechanisms. One aspect of economic reality repairs a flaw located in another aspect of the same reality. In every aspect of this reality, as in the division of labor, in monopoly, etc., there is a good and a bad side. Economy does not automatically balance itself, in the way that classical or modern liberalism thought that "forces balance one another." Yet there is no need to do away with the existing economic reality completely; the good must be maintained by purifying it of the evil. Here Marx argued against Proudhon that, even though his position is one of "this as well as that," it is not a dialectical position, and Marx was correct.

Proudhon's theory takes the form of harmonious structure, and the corrective character of his social theory is anchored in harmonizing approach. What does the corrective nature of his theory involve? In a given reality, the seeds of a more desirable reality are to be found. Reality must be assisted in revealing these seeds. Human reason functions as a mediator for this reality by way of a mediation of a surgeon who uproots the evil inherent in sickness, or as the crutches that will give a proper poise to reality.

The dialectic of Marx and Hegel stands in contradistinction to this view, and Marx fully accepted the dialectic in this context. The dialectic implies functions within reality and manifests itself in the antithesis of reality, not in the balancing of reality. Therefore, reason does not mediate from without but operates from within reality as it drives it on to new stages by exposing its antithesis. The solution by way of opposites is not in their balancing but in their forward progression as implied in the eleventh thesis. Now the harmonistic approach, that serves as a foundation to the corrective character of his social theory can be distinguished from the dialectic approach that serves as a foundation to the revolutionary viewpoint. The concept of reason for Marx was not a *surgical* concept, returning to the figurative language used above. His concept was *organistic*. It points out an inner growth from inner sources, the rhythm of which is that of opposites, which reach their full manifestation in a condition of change achieved through the progression of history to its next stage.

One historical detail adequately explained for Marx the difference between himself and Proudhon. This is to be found in his 1856 letter to Johann Baptist von Schweitzer, a German politician and writer. Marx said that Proudhon gave the strong impression, that according to Proudhon, as according to Kant, the solution of antinomies denoted something beyond the human mind, that is, something that remained obscure to the human mind. The aspect of this remark that contains a personal attack against the insufficient insight of Proudhon must be disregarded, for Marx argued that the objective limitations of knowledge according to Kant are actually the individual limitations of the insight of Proudhon. The point is that Marx wanted to stress that, according to Proudhon, contradictions, or the antinomies, do not find their solution in the progress of history or reality. The antinomies are beyond reality. In opposition to this, Marx held that the antinomies that arise in reality find their solution within reality, but the reality after the solution is a different stage then the stage of the antinomies themselves. We remain within the boundaries of reality, but, because this reality is dynamic and the rhythm of the dynamic is the rhythm of progression from one stage to the next, the antinomy at one stage finds its solution at the following stage. This difference between the harmonistic and the dialectic approaches is of central importance to the understanding of the sources of the Marxian theory of philosophy. But which antinomies history reconciles becomes a critical question. Possibly the antinomies that are historical are reconciled, such as the antithesis between labor and property, or between ownership of the resources of man, and labor with resources. But can it be said that history is capable of reconciling contradictions that are not *merely* historical, such as the antithesis between man as a creature and the world surrounding him, to which he belongs and yet with which he cannot be identified? Or can even antitheses that include less be reconciled, such as the antithesis between the individual and the whole, or the will of the individual and the ability given him? The maintenance of Marx's theory implies that everything is history—this has already been shown—but the idea is repeated throughout the discussion. It reaches its climax in a decisive statement: "M. Proudhon does not know that the whole of history is nothing but a continual transformation of human nature" (page 160). Did Marx on the basis of actual inquiry have the authority to say this? Did he have the authority to interpret the changes, which he correctly considers to be changes in human *nature?* When he wrote his book against Proudhon, Marx forgot a vitally important comment he had made in his "Manuscripts," i.e., that man has innate powers, his intelligence and physical fitness for labor. Also forces and talents exist by which labor can be divided between different people, including the ability to exchange mutual services.[5]

In this statement Marx clearly distinguishes between historical and nonhistorical factors. He gives intelligence as one nonhistorical factor, assuming the capacity of the reason of man, an ability without which practice ceases to function as the practical activity of man. We are faced here with the fundamental paradox of the Marxian theory. Marx maintained the dialectical view, because he saw in it the expression of the nature of reason. But he did not provide an explanation of the rational character of history when he eliminated the rational nature of man, which is not merely a historical occurrence, like the changing economic and social conditions. This rational nature of man is the logical and metaphysical asumption of the rational nature of history. Marx was hesitant to conclude in this manner. He set up history as a total reality and erased the meta-historical nature of man (or man's intelligence). He did away with the fulcrum of the idea by stating that history is rational and capable, with the aid of the dialectic movement, of solving its own problems. How did it happen that history is more rational than man who is its creator? Marx could not explain this if he held to the idea that the nature of man is itself an historical creation, that man's reason is just a product of history. Marx preferred to formulate his idea of the nature of man in a radical historical manner, because "rationality" was so evident from a relevant personal standpoint as well as from the standpoint of the history of ideas. However, it cannot be said philosophically that reason, the subject of philosophy and its instrument of inquiry, is to be taken for granted. History cannot be made independent of the reason of man as does the radical historicist interpretation being considered here. To add to the paradox, this is the point of greatest alienation of man from himself. Once Marx attributed to history, as a pro-

[5] *MEGA,* I, 3, p. 141; Marx, "Economic and Philosophical Manuscripts," trans. T. B. Bottomore, in Erich Fromm, *Marx's Concept of Man* (New York: Frederick Ungar, 1961), p. 158.

duct of practice, more reason than he attributed to man himself, he only increased the self-alienation of man. Thus the historicism of Marx amounted eventually to alienation. But Marx did not apply the test of criticism to it as he did to the fetish-alienation in economics. It does not seem to be accidental that he did not deal with this basic alienation that his historicism in all its radical manifestations denotes; for alienation-of-facts in economics can be eliminated by revolution; but alienation-of-consciousness, that is, the making of history independent of the nature of man, cannot be eliminated by revolution. The latter can only be eliminated by another consciousness, by philosophy. But Marx wanted to materialize the current impoverished, abstract, and mystery-prone philosophy. Is it possible to materialize such a philosophy? Can consciousness be realized completely? It is evidently impossible, for reason and the activity of consciousness are always more than all their manifestations. The materialization of philosophy, similar to that of reason, is likely to lead to Marxian conclusions, with an elimination of reason itself or an elimination of man's nature in terms of reason, hence placing man in a state of historical flux. It must be concluded that philosophy, which is the contemplation of reason by reason, cannot be materialized. Therefore, what Marx accomplished was nothing but the eradication of philosophy, illegitimately represented as its realization. The relation between the nature of man and history evinces a weakness in Marx. His attempt to materialize philosophy was actually a *tour de force*.

In this same context the relation of Marx to the dialectic is essential. The common opinion that Marx accepted the dialectical method and then deserted the system in which this method was crystallized has no foundation. This can be explained by referring to Hegel. Method, Hegel said, is consciousness of the independent inner movement of content.[6] Here Hegel formulated the relation between method and the content that the method reveals. Method is not a tool that

[6] Georg Hegel, *Wissenschaft der Logik* (Leipzig: Felix Meiner, 1923), I, p. 35.

once having been used for discovering content can then be discarded. Method is nothing but the manifestation of content that is itself structured to contain contraries. Hence, the dialectical method cannot be separated from dialectical contents. Marx did not separate them, for he tried to show that history contains historical contents that reveal themselves in history. Dialectical theory is concerned with discovering what there is in reality. But actually Marx narrowed the scope of the method. For Hegel, the rational method was the manifestation of the rational content. But whence does this content derive its rationality? When the contents are not claimed to be rational, it cannot be said that the method will be rational when referring to the dialectical method. Therefore, Hegel said elsewhere that method is itself a concept, which knows itself and is its own object.[7]

The dialectic method is not divisible from the concepts to which it applies, since it is not external like an experimental model, in which, for instance, the metal to be smelted does not necessarily reflect the method used to effect its smelting, that is, the iron smelted does not call for this or that smelting instrument.

When Marx assumed the rational dialectical character of history, he could use the rational method in referring to history. Precisely because of this assumption he could presuppose the "organistic" view of reason. If this were not so, he would have had no way out but to rely upon the external mediation of reason and could not have used the dialectical method. Therefore, the use of this method was no more than a manifestation of Marx's first assumption of the rational nature of man, which contradicts his historicist formulations, such as the formulation of the historical character of the nature of man, which served to initiate this discussion.

Optimism. Marx's formulation of the dialectical view is noteworthy: "That in the same relations in which wealth is produced, poverty is produced also; that in the same relations in

[7] Hegel, *Wissenschaft der Logik,* II, p. 486.

which there is a development of productive forces, there is a productive force of repression; that these relations produce bourgeois wealth, that is to say, the wealth of the bourgeois class, only in continually annihilating the wealth of integral members of that class and in producing an ever-growing proletariat" (page 134). The reconciliation of dialectical contraries admits the progression of history to its next stage, to the stage of "progress without anarchy" (page 78). It seems that herein Marx's historical view and historical optimism were expressed. The progression of history is not only progression to a new stage, but also to a more advanced stage, since antinomies that were once existent are now reconciled. The reconciliation of these antinomies solves the problem inherent in them as well, such as the problem of the contradiction between the development of production and the degeneration of the workers who work for it. Marx gave a most radical form to the process of reconciliation when he spoke about the *ultimate* reconciliation. The word "ultimate" gives the idea of progression and advance an eschatological tone, a tone of the world to come. From the analysis undertaken here, however, it seems that the tone of eschatology is confined to the field of discourse, the realm of economic-social history alone. The main point is the historical progression itself. This optimism is merely the transfer of the dialectical idea of Hegel to history. Every stage in concept formation was, for Hegel, a richer stage then the former one, because it included the previous stages, revealing an additional content of reason. Marx attached a certain historical significance to this principle. Historical progression is historical advancement because it solves problems left unsolved in the previous historical stage, and basically because it opens up a field of activity to the depressed. It makes the depressed active subjects of history instead of the enslaved and passive creatures they were in the preceding stage of history. The criterion of relevant historical moral progression is connected with the analysis of history according to the absolute standard of the position of man as subject. The optimistic analysis of history according to the criterion of progression is not possible without this assumption, that a metaphysical and moral nature exists in man that manifests itself in history. We inquire into history and propose statements with the assumption in mind that the nature of man materializes or ceases to materialize within it. It is doubtful whether Marx could maintain his attitude and hold that the realm of metaphysics and that of history are identical.

The optimism in the idea of progression in Marx's theory manifests itself in another idea as well. "The division of labor in the automatic factory is characterised by this, that labor there has lost all specialised character. But from the moment that all special development ceases, the need of universality, the tendency towards an integral development of the individual begins to make itself felt. The automatic factory effaces species and the stupefying of handicraft" (page 157). The optimism in this statement can be discussed sociologically. It could be argued that the preindustrial stage was marred by the absence of narrow specialization. It could also be held that the "second industrial revolution" will bring about a broadening of horizons. Yet it is clear that the present economic stage engenders specialization, assembly lines, and automation. Sociological criticism is not, however, the basic issue at hand. The main point in this context is what has been called dialectical optimism, "that when special development ceases, the need of universality makes itself felt." When one aim has established itself, another complementary and opposing stage is called upon immediately.

This optimism was formulated in an extensive manner in Marx's letter to Annenkow (December 28, 1846), in which Marx wrote that, "men never relinquish what they have won, but this does not mean that they never relinquish the social form in which they have acquired certain productive forces. On the contrary, in order that they may not be deprived of the result attained and forfeit the fruits of civilization, they are obliged, from the moment when the form of the *commerce* no longer corresponds to the productive forces acquired, to change all their traditional social forms."[8] In this important quotation, Marx expressed several things: (1) There is an accumulation of accomplishments that the next historical stage does not renounce and dispose of but preserves in a new form. (2) There is a distinction between the thing and its form; it is in this, in the matter of economic achievements, that Marx maintained the distinction between content and form that was previously ignored in the discussion of the nature of man. (3) In the progress from one historical stage to another, the teleological factor comes to the fore: "in order . . . not to be deprived of . . . the fruits of civilization." The dialectical movement that is the result of certain necessary causes is by the same token a result of the necessity of ends. The appearance of the movement through opposites and also through ends is sufficient to serve the purpose of the preservation of the achievements of civilization. The determination of a place for the teleological rhythm raises another question: What is the role of the conscious judgments of man? For it is clearly these judgments that seek the preservation of the achievements of civilization. But Marx did not deal with this most important subject in this letter.

Author and Artist. After a critical examination of the ideas of Marx, the consideration of his several famous formulations in *The Poverty of Philosophy* can serve as a key for the understanding of his doctrine in general. Even though they contain nothing novel or not dealt with previously, they do effectively elucidate his doctrine.

"In constructing with the categories of political economy the edifice of an ideological system, the members of the social system are dislocated. The different members of society are changed as belonging to separate societies which arrive one after the other. How, indeed, can the single logical formula of movement, of succession, of time, explain the composition

[8] Karl Marx and Friedrich Engels, *Correspondence, 1846–1895* (New York: International Publishers, n.d.), p. 8.

of society, in which all the relations co-exist simultaneously and support each other?" (page 120). In this statement, Marx said that any particular factor cannot be singled out from the social circle, such as the categorical factor, as illustrated by Proudhon. However, the same question can be asked of Marx himself, who viewed social reality as a system. Nevertheless, in the historical process he gave decisive preference to the economic factor. He evidently realized the existing dependence of all factors upon the economic. Perhaps the view of Marx in this statement, which urges one social realm, is to be preferred to his specific teaching of historical or practical materialism.[9]

Marx presented his historical-human theory in a striking statement already referred to: "But from the moment that you represent men as the actors and the authors of their own history you have, by a detour, arrived at the actual point of departure since you have abandoned the eternal principles from which you first set out" (page 125). On this, reference can be made to the elucidation of the third thesis on Feuerbach. An interpretation of the same idea in a different perspective is the formulation that the forces of production are the product of the energy of man. However, this energy is itself limited by the circumstances in which men are bound and by the forces of production already explained by the form of society preceding them, which are not circumstances of its formation but are the effects of the previous generation. The example citing the actors exemplifies the activity and to a certain extent also the freedom of man; the example of artists serves clearly to project the passivity as well as the enslavement of man. But this dependence is a dependence upon human history from the standpoint of the accumulation of the forms of production and the forces of production that have reached the present generation from the inheritance of the past. The limitation of freedom is historical, and the free activity of man is again an outcome of historical forces. This is an expression of the contraction of the scope of freedom and the substitution of the

[9] See Nathan Rotenstreich, *Between Past and Present: An Essay on History* (New Haven: Yale University Press, 1958), pp. 135–136.

relation between man and his history, as well as the transfer to history of the sphere of freedom from its relation between man and the entire universe.

A kind of play-of-forces within humanity is pointed up here also. For the past that provides restraints and circumstances to the active powers of the present is a human past; hence, it cannot be argued that man is subordinated to a compelling law, the law of nature. The law governing human behavior derives from the existing human circumstances and is the law of the acts of man done in the past; hence, to a certain degree, it can be expropriated by man's activity in the present. This activity exists forever, but in each generation it is involved with the circumstances of the previous generation. Therefore, Marx believed in the continuity of humanity, in terms of its activity, and the limitation of this continuity by the power gained from what is already accomplished. Finally, Marx argued that there is a place for the activity of the present even though he admitted its limitations. The idea of the dramatists must be interpreted as well as the acting; man has freedom even though it is limited. This statement is apparently a sign of Marx's determinism, on which he is often quoted and of which he is often accused. However, this is merely a half-truth.

The limited freedom of man as the subject of action appears to be mentioned in Marx's argument against Proudhon, but it is valid for Hegel as well. For Hegel, man was a tool, serving the idea of eternal reason for the sake of development and progression. It is of the utmost importance to emphasize at this point the objection to the idea of man as a tool. We can learn from it that Marx did not believe at all that on the basis of his theory man becomes an instrument in the hands of historical dialectical and economic progress. It would seem that the idea that "progress is for the sake of man, to preserve the achievements of civilization" could eliminate the fear Marx had that he himself was making man into an instrument to be used by nonhuman forces. It would seem also that Marx was of the opinion that the fact that man engages in the activity of freedom and the fact that the objective development of history is itself for the sake of active man do not leave room for the interpretation that he believed man has become enslaved through external forces.

At this point a line can be drawn separating Marx and Marxism, especially in respect to the Bolshevist version of Marxism. When Marx spoke of progress for the sake of man, or of the activity of freedom, he evidently did not identify progress or civilization with a particular state and regime, as Bolshevism does. Moreover, Marx set his philosophical development apart by criticizing the position attributed to the state in Hegel's philosophy, while Bolshevism clearly reestablishes, as opposed to Marx's view, the fundamental importance of the state.

The elucidation of the concept of activity depends on the fundamental distinction between the class itself and the class for itself (page 189). The basis for this distinction is to be found in Hegelian terminology, in which a distinction was made between the objective status of a thing (in itself) and the condition in which consciousness is simultaneous to that which is given objectively (for itself). It was Marx's fundamental assumption that man is his own dramatic author and, furthermore, that the fact or basis of activity is retained in the consciousness accompanying historical activities. The class that knows its place within the drama of history reaches the level of class for itself. Finally, this also served as a foothold for the Marxian critique of political economics. This explanation may be prefaced with the observation that political economics as the science about man is connected with the assumption that the forces of production are the substance of human existence. In order to give to political economics, as a science, the central task that Marx attributed to it, the subject matter of this science in terms of economic relations must necessarily be seen as the substance of human existence. The subject matter of economics inherits the place held by the traditional subject matter of metaphysics. On this assumption, the science of economics claims to be the inheritor of philosophy. On the other hand, economic life must be viewed as historical. This consideration would serve as a basis for the argument that when we deal with economic life we are dealing with history. And this, according to Marx, was dealing with the nature of man.

This subject matter is *the* subject matter, and the laws operating within it are historical and nonnatural. Arguing that the subject matter is natural and not historical is not a scientific, but an ideological, error, since it is not founded upon a lack of understanding. Therefore, Marx said that economists are the scientific representatives of the bourgeois class. He drew a parallel between those who engage in economics and the socialists and communists, who are the theoretical representatives of the proletariat class. It cannot be said that Marx was fair toward the political economists in making them servants to the class and in denying their analysis and findings as ideological. The proof is that his relation to Ricardo cannot be reconciled with his inclusive condemnation of political economics as ideology. There was, in truth, no need for Marx to say that they do not understand the historical nature of economics and that they are the ideologists of the bourgeois class. But this is the way in which Marx thought, and it engaged him in polemic and in the radical formulation of his findings.

In Marx's essay against Proudhon, the statement is found also that the political regime is an official expression of the antithesis in bourgeois society (page 120). This was repeated in *The Communist Manifesto,* in which Marx said that up to now the development of society was connected with political revolutions, but with the final reconciliation of the antitheses of society this connection will cease. This did not imply the idea of the withering away of the state, yet perhaps it contained a relevant statement of the same idea formulated with a degree of caution.

DETERMINATION OF CONSCIOUSNESS BY EXISTENCE

In several writings, Marx expressed the concept of the determination of consciousness by life or by existence. The analysis of the "Theses on Feuerbach," as well as the polemic against Proudhon, make the importance of this view for Marx's philosophy clear.[10] A critical analysis of this view reveals not only the position of this thesis in Marx's theory but also its popularity in the general climate of opinion of our time and the place it occupies as a slogan.

Activity and Contents. First and foremost, it must be stressed that Marx could not assume that the activity of consciousness as such is derived from existence, although his argument sometimes sounds as if he assumed this. He himself said that economic activity is fully permeated with consciousness. Yet he maintained that the activity of consciousness is derived from the realm of economic activity when the latter is already permeated with the former. Hence, the functional aspect of consciousness, consciousness as activity, must be assumed by Marx and be understood to be present in every manifestation of human activity, including the economic. It may be questioned whether Marx was consistent on this point and whether he clarified for himself the various features of the concept or sphere of consciousness.

As opposed to the genetic views that attempt to derive a human phenomenon (which consciousness certainly is) from a reality that is not solely human, Marx from the first confined his analysis to the human domain. He tried to show only how human reality, social and historical, determines the content of the presupposed activity of consciousness. His purpose, to use again his own expression, was to show that it is existence that determines consciousness, and not consciousness that determines existence.

Marx was interested in human reality, which he identified

[10] The relevant text reads: "The mode of production in material life determines the general character of the social, political and spiritual processes of life. It is not the consciousness of men that determines their existence, but on the contrary, their social existence determines their consciousness." Marx, *A Contribution to the Critique of Political Economy*, trans. N. I. Stone (Chicago: C. H. Kerr, 1911), pp. 11–12.

with the social-historical process. He identified existence with the existence of society, and because he accepted Hegel's theory that "subjective spirit" is present only in individuals, Marx related consciousness to the individual. Bearing these points in mind, his assertion that existence determines consciousness may be interpreted by substituting "society" for the former factor and "the individual" for the latter. In other words, Marx's assertion must be interpreted as follows: reality or existence qua social determines the contents and norms, or world outlooks, broadly speaking, that individual consciousness entertains in its activity.

Underlying Marx's conception of reality as society was his desire to show how one characteristic feature of human existence, the social and historical process, determines another, namely, man's world outlook. According to Marx, the characteristic features of human existence at both levels, reality and world outlook, are intimately related by virtue of the causative or, more cautiously, determinative power of the former vis-à-vis the latter. However, does it necessarily follow from the fact that one human factor determines another that man's every outlook, especially regarding nature, is determined by historical and social reality? In order to assume this, the independent position of what might be called observation or contemplation, which comprises research, awareness, understanding, the posing of questions, and so on, must be negated. Marx's criticism of philosophy qua speculation amounts to a negation of this position of contemplation (eleventh thesis). But the human attitude of observation or contemplation is but the expression of the activity of consciousness and as such cannot be regarded as partially or totally determined by social and historical reality. Marx himself assumed that the activity of consciousness as such is not derived from reality, and to be consistent he should have allowed room for contemplation. By so doing, however, he would have overstepped the framework of his premises on the determinability of consciousness by existence and his denial of a certain independence of philosophy proper.

If Marx wanted to imply that consciousness (in terms of its views and norms) is determined exclusively by historical reality, he had to presuppose its lack of any spontaneous urge, as expressed in such activities as contemplation and observation. Accordingly, even posing questions, searching for answers, and examining reality must be considered as aspects of consciousness determined by its dependence upon reality. This would be a far-reaching conclusion, amounting to the absolute negation of consciousness as an independent activity.

Furthermore, in order to assume that historical and social reality determines consciousness and the views held in it, the capacity of consciousness to function for the sake of social human existence must be assumed. The views and norms are, in this case, tools or instruments employed for the sake of reality. However, according to Marx's own view, it is clear that in the absence of a conscious activity historical reality itself would not come into existence. Thus, while consciousness as an independent activity has to some extent the power of creating reality, at the same time, as regards its own views, it is subservient to this reality. Yet Marx did not even pose, let alone answer, the question of how consciousness, while having some creative or productive power, creating or participating in the creation of historical or economic productivity, is at the same time only derivative and instrumental with regard to its position toward this reality. Did Marx think that the creative or productive power of consciousness exhausted itself in the very production of the initial stages of human economic activity and that consequently there is no room for further and progressive expressions of this creative power in terms of such functions as maintaining the contemplative position or formulating world outlooks and norms?

Instrument. In order to assume that consciousness is an instrument in the service of historical reality, two prior assumptions must be made, although they are not explicitly posited by Marx: (1) Consciousness is bound to know the reality that it serves as an instrument, for if it did not, it would not be in a position to fulfill its function adequately. However, its knowledge of reality implies that consciousness features an independent aspect of knowing, the activity of contemplation and observation. Hence, instrumentality cannot be attributed to consciousness without first assuming that it is inherently capable of observation, contemplation, and knowledge. (2) It must be acknowledged that consciousness is characterized by the specific ability to respond to the needs of reality. Consciousness knows reality and, furthermore, lends itself to respond to the needs directed to it by reality. This being the case, response to reality cannot be assumed to be simply a relationship of determination by a causative power, or a one-way relationship from reality to consciousness. Response to reality is rather a highly complicated relationship in which at least two aspects can be distinguished, that of understanding reality served by consciousness and that of adopting a position of serving it. In other words, in order to assume with Marx that historical and social reality determine consciousness, at least an additional relation between consciousness and reality must be taken for granted, consisting not simply of a causative determination. Summing up, it may be said that consciousness that does not contemplate reality by way of cognition and recognition and that lacks an independent urge is also unable to respond to the needs stemming from this reality. Consciousness, in order to serve and become a result of reality, must be possessed of an inner capacity, independent of the reality it serves as an instrument. The very fact that it can transcend reality critically implies, at least, that consciousness is partially independent.

Mirroring and Justifying. In a more detailed interpretation of the idea of the determinability of consciousness by reality, two possible meanings of the relationship between reality and consciousness can be suggested: (1) The domain of contents, views, and norms may be conceived as a reflection or a mirror of given, factual reality. For example, we may say that slavery exists in reality, while consciousness explains slavery by referring it to a meaningful context in the attempt to establish its justification in terms of the stratification of and differences between human beings; or else we may say that private property exists in reality, and consciousness, by its own methods, states that private property is a necessary feature or right of human reality. (2) The determinability or instrumentality of consciousness might also imply that it serves reality by justifying it. This applies, for instance, to cases in which the legal system protects private property, or in which a political philosophy presents private property as the expression of man's natural rights, or shows slavery to be an essential part of human reality by positing a fundamental distinction between beings who are tools and people who are free persons.

The first interpretation of the idea of determinability may be omitted because it involves an obvious difficulty; it would be very difficult to show that a particular framework of conscious contents mirrors social or historical reality. At the most, it can be asserted that some aspects of a historical reality do find their expression in a framework of contents. Thus, according to this line of reasoning, expressed in Marxist literature, the central position assigned to freedom by Kant reflected the historical fact of the French Revolution.[11] But even of this example, it may be said that Kant's fundamental intuition, as it were, was the idea of the human being deciding freely about his behavior. Moreover, closer consideration reveals that the actual setting of the system is far more complicated and, as such, not to be interpreted by means of a simple identification with a historical event, which at most finds only partial expression in it. This example was chosen only in order to show that the interpretation that reduces the determinability of consciousness to the idea that it reflects reality is, to say the least, primitive and certainly cannot account for all the shades of reasoning and points of view found in a philosophical system.

[11] In "The German Ideology" Marx related Kant's notion of the good will to the social position of the German bourgeoisie and its lack of power of realization; *MEGA,* I, 5, p. 175.

The interpretation that attributes the determinability of consciousness to its function as an instrument in the service of historical and social reality is more cautious than the former, so that it can, as such, be taken more seriously. For the sake of analysis, it may be assumed either that the very domain of thoughts, values, and principles originally came into existence only for the sake of the historical reality or that this domain's existence is taken for granted for the above or for other reasons. As a matter of fact, however, the contents of consciousness also perform a social function, being instruments in the service of social and historical reality. These two interpretations assume that historical reality needs the instrument of thoughts, ideas and values without explaining *why*. What impoverishes historical reality, or puts it in need to such an extent that it must be compensated in the domain of consciousness through the medium of its ideas and values? It is perhaps necessary to assume a fundamental relationship between reality and consciousness, or between man and consciousness, which is therefore in a position to serve his needs. This being the case, man can turn to consciousness in order to employ it as an instrument in and for his social and historical reality.

Thus, from a closer examination of the idea of the instrumentality of consciousness vis-à-vis reality, it follows that consciousness is able to fulfill its function only because it possesses as such something that reality lacks. Returning for a moment to what was hinted at in one of the examples above, Aristotle's philosophy, rather than being confined to a description of slavery as a given feature of Greek society, also justified its existence. Let us now suppose, with the Marxists, that justification in this or similar cases is not the outcome of an inner rhythm or logic of philosophical thinking, but rather serves the purposes of reality by safeguarding and upholding what actually exists. Granted this, it still must be acknowledged that the very activity of suggesting, justifying, or reasoning is not present in the opaque historical reality, but rather stems from the inherent nature of consciousness facing reality. From the point of view of its subject matter, the ideology of such a philosophical system as the Aristotelian, as well as of others, conforms with reality by virtue of dealing with slavery (or other matters) as phenomena of reality, and by providing justification for these phenomena within the scope of reality. From another point of view, there is no conformity between reality and ideology, because the latter raises the subject matter of its consideration to a meaningful plane of its own; slavery ceases to be a mere fact and becomes a phenomenon demanding and gaining authorization, justification, and moral status. Hence the difference can be realized between the domain of historical reality and that of consciousness or ideology, which is manifest in the different characteristics attributed within each to the fact of slavery. The very activity of justification, demonstration, or accounting for, even when concerned with reality, is neither dependent on, nor derived from, any specific historical content and can therefore be applied to any kind of content.

True, justification may serve ideological ends and this constitutes falsification of the facts, as is the case when conceptual and moral means are employed to vindicate what does not merit vindication. However, even an invalid ideological vindication can be accomplished only because the activity of justification is not confined to the specific content to which it is applied. Thus, in this context there are no grounds for positing a one-way determinability, that is to say, determination of consciousness by existence. Here a meeting between the two domains is encountered, a meeting in which the activity of consciousness is not entirely dependent on reality and upon the contents to which it refers. Above, the necessity of presupposing a responsive activity inherent in consciousness was shown, if the assumption of its instrumentality were to be plausible. It may be added now that were it not for the activity of justification, a manifestation of consciousness, consciousness would neither constitute an instrument of reality nor be capable of fulfilling even the very limited function attributed to it by the Marxist doctrine.

An even more general view may be ventured here. Man needs ideological justification because his relation to reality is governed essentially by a selected criterion of justification. Because human consciousness is concerned not only with the given factual aspects of reality, but also with whether or not reality conforms to criteria, it may be assumed that man has an ideology in the Marxist sense, that is, he employs ideas improperly. Metaphorically speaking, ideology constitutes blundering or myopia and not blindness; yet to be short-sighted, man must first of all have eyes capable of seeing. Returning to the conceptual analysis: the duality between the given facts and the standards governing our relation to them is fundamental and universal; thus standards, norms, and principles cannot be derived from any historical reality, being merely a reflection of it.

Suppressed Sovereignty. Having pointed out the difficulties involved in the idea of the determinability of consciousness by historical reality, it must now be added that according to the Marxist view this determination exists only in that stage of history wherein overwhelming weight is attributed to interests, that is to say, in the era of private property. The dependence of consciousness on social reality is actually a characteristic of human enslavement, being an expression of man's self-estrangement. A state wherein consciousness is totally dependent on reality and ideologically serves economic interests constitutes a deviation from the right order of things. Therefore, historical reality is a process toward emancipation of humanity and the consequent correction of the deviation; in "the reign of freedom" there will be no dependence of this sort. Consciousness will face reality as an independent factor. In short, Marx held that: (a) consciousness as a matter of principle is sovereign vis-à-vis reality and, as such, is a manifestation of man's freedom; and (b) as a matter of fact, in human reality as it is, there is an inverted relation between the two, because man's subjugation to his own product-making is essentially the enslavement of consciousness by reality.

In criticizing this theory, the plausibility of attributing to historical reality a decisive power capable of reversing the essentially independent position of consciousness vis-à-vis reality must be questioned. To be sure, Marx assigned decisive significance to historical reality, because it is a specific attribute of human existence. Historical reality, however, did not come into existence without the active participation of consciousness. It is in history that man transcends nature as it is given, even according to Marx, and this very transcendence presupposes the independent activity of consciousness, although this Marx did not assume. Man, who created history, released himself to some extent from the facts of nature and created a new level of reality which, according to Marx's view, in turn enslaves the consciousness that underlies it.

There is no need to deal at this juncture with the specific historical conception expressed in the Marxist outline; the discussion may be confined to the philosophical principle implied by it. Let us put it this way: How is the power of factual historical reality to reverse a fundamental structure to be understood? Or how is it possible for consciousness, which is fundamentally independent, to become dependent and even enslaved? Let us examine some factual conditions under which man's fundamental capacity might possibly be obliterated or at least diminished. Take, for example, a human being deprived of human society and living among animals, who consequently does not develop his linguistic capacity. In this case, the human being's capacity is not obliterated but merely dormant, because of the absence of the conditions requisite for its actualization. Is the distorted relationship of consciousness to reality, the enslavement of humanity, likewise the result of factual (in this case historical) conditions precluding the actualization of man's freedom? Another relevant example may be found in the psychopathological sphere: it is said that because man is endowed with consciousness, he is independent, for consciousness enables him to maintain contact with both past and future. When his mental equipment or his brain is impaired, man's consciousness may become confined to the present moment and lose its fundamental capacity to enlarge the scope of his time-perspective. Is the enslavement of man's essentially free consciousness likewise due to mental damage, wrought by historical conditions? Obviously, the first example, concerning the absence of the conditions requisite for the realization of man's linguistic capacity, applies only to rare individual cases, and as such can hardly further the understanding of universal historical processes. In order to assign to history the force of prohibitive conditions, based on the pattern of what happens to an individual, one must first attribute to it the power to deprive humanity of the very capacity that created history. For, according to Marx himself, history would not have being, were it not for the creative power of consciousness. Furthermore, the fundamental human capacity, freedom, is already manifest within human scope. How can history turn against its own creator? While it is true that historical reality does not manifest the capacity of freedom in its full inner momentum, it is not true that historical reality obliterates this capacity completely. The same can be said for the second example: Consciousness, though damaged in the scope of an individual, still persists in the scope of mankind in general. According to the Marxist view, in historical reality as it is, consciousness is totally immersed in the facts and no longer maintains its independent position opposite to or above the facts. Accordingly, the fundamental and normative relationships between consciousness and reality are reversed.

However, reality does not possess this power of total annihilation; it cannot preclude man's activity in the domain of principles or, in our case, in the sphere of moral imperatives and values. The only possible and factual relationship between man and mind consists in man's employment of the spiritual façade as an instrument for authorizing or sanctioning reality. If the Marxist idea that the power of reality reverses the fundamental structure is denied, however, it may be assumed that even in reality as it is, there is at least some spiritual independence or, conversely, that reality does not totally subjugate the domain of principles and mind. The authority and guidance of the principles does not, therefore, constitute a new birth. Consciousness in itself is not a historical fact and, being outside the historical realm, can neither be attacked nor obliterated by historical facts, nor can the recovery of its status be contingent upon the coming of a new historical reality based, to use Marxist terms, on freedom as against necessity. Consciousness is an essential attribute of any man and is active in any historical reality. Historical reality can, at the most, occasion and permit, to some extent, the guiding activity of consciousness.

The denial of the Marxist thesis that consciousness and freedom are fundamentally reversed in reality has bearing on social reality, in that it excludes the assumption of a total gap between the factual and the eschatological situations, between present and future. Relationship to and guidance by spiritual contents are essential attributes of human nature. Man, by virtue of his consciousness, is characterized by a relationship to contents and values. Actual human life borders on the subjective and the objective, and within this sphere man is capable of looking beyond the object as such; in other words, he is capable of responding to contents that occupy his consciousness. From this premiss we cannot arrive at Marx's conclusion. Consciousness, although manifest in history, cannot be entirely determined by it. Man takes two steps beyond given reality: by the first he creates history and human reality, and by the second he transcends history and maintains his resonance toward contents. The same consciousness that creates history possesses the capacity to respond to what is not merely historical, to values and contents. Man is a spiritual being by virtue of his very reality, which contains its own self-transcendence. Transcendence of nature is an integral aspect of the factual existence of consciousness and is perpetually manifested in the creation of history. Transcendence of history and maintenance of contact with the realm of principles is likewise an essential attribute of consciousness. It is only through the taking of both steps toward transcendence that the specific nature of human existence becomes salient.[12]

The perverted relationship of consciousness with reality amounting to the subjugation of consciousness is the core of the phenomenon called *alienation* or *self-alienation*. Next, this phenomenon will be dealt with in its intellectual context.

[12] *See* Rotenstreich, *Spirit and Man.*

CHAPTER 7

Concept of Alienation and Its Metamorphoses

In the preceding analysis reference had to be made time and again to the phenomenon of alienation or self-alienation of man. It became clear that this phenomenon occupies a central position in Marx's system, in his criticism of society, and in his view of the total change society is due to make. It seems appropriate now to deal specifically with this phenomenon. Some light might be thrown on it by tracing the changing contents of this concept.

Over the ages, the term "alienation" [1] has been used in several different senses. In our own day, the term has found widespread usage and figures prominently in two contexts. The first context is psychological or psychiatric. In this, "alienation" denotes two classes of psychic phenomena: (a) the loss of personal identity or the radical conversion of personality; and (b) loneliness, self-isolation from, or loss of contact with others and society, as well as the replacement of emotional reactions and relations by a callous, mechanical attitude.[2] When used in the second context, the one that bears traces of Marx's influence, the term alienation denotes the process whereby the object produced by men's work comes to be regarded as stand-

[1] *Entfremdung* or *Entäusserung,* in German.

[2] Rollo May, "Contributions to Existential Psychotherapy," in *Existence: A New Dimention in Psychiatry and Psychology,* ed. Rollo May, Ernest Angel, and Henri Ellenberger (New York: Basic Books, 1958), pp. 56 ff.

ing over and against (as alienated from) the workers and their work. In this case, production is the transfer of work to the realm of objects (*Vergegenständlichung*) and the abolishment of the reality (*Entwirklichung*) of the worker.[3]

CURRENT USAGE

Underlying both of these current connotations of the alienation concept is the basic juridical meaning of the Latin term *"alienatio,"* namely, the transfer or conveyance of property to another. Yet even in classical antiquity the concept of alienation carried another connotation, the proper context of which was the sphere of the soul. Thus the expression *"alienatio mentis"* was used to signify insanity or loss of control over one's psychic and intellectual faculties. The notion that evidently stands behind the use of the term *"alienatio"* to denote psychopathological phenomena is that insanity consists in an internal dissolution or fission of the soul, which results, as it were, in the separation of the soul's faculties from one another and their alienation from personal identity. Perhaps the modern psychiatric connotation of "alienation" may be regarded as an extension of the original connotation of *"alienatio mentis,"* provided it is realized that the modern term denotes a wider, less definite range of phenomena than the ancient one.

Be this as it may, what is of particular interest from a philosophical viewpoint is the conceptual background of the other modern meaning of "alienation," namely, the meaning first ascribed to it by Marx. It would therefore be worth while to survey several different philosophical contexts in which the concept of alienation has figured, with a view to determining the systematic differences between the stages of this concept's metamorphosis.

[3] Karl Marx, "Ökonomische-Philosophische Manuskripte, 1844," *MEGA* I, 3, p. 83; Marx, "Economic and Philosophical Manuscripts," trans. T. B. Bottomore, in Erich Fromm, *Marx's Concept of Man* (New York: Frederick Ungar, 1961), p. 95.

EKSTASIS

The Latin term *"alienatio"* corresponds to the Greek term ἀλλοίωσις, which in turn corresponds to still another Greek term, ἔκστασις. Just as *"ekstasis"* connotes the state of being beside oneself or transported from one's self, so *"alienatio"* means the state of being of a man who, having been beside himself, is transformed into another. It is this merger of meaning that underlies the use of the term *"alienatio"* or ἀλλοίωσις to signify that change as a result of which a man is alienated from himself, transported from himself to become submerged in God or in the One.

Plotinus defined true contemplation in this way as a state of being in which the soul, having lost consciousness of itself and no longer differentiated from the One, becomes other than and estranged from itself. Using the term θεωρία to denote the contemplating soul's loss of concepts and forms, Plotinus characterized the culmination of contemplation as a state of alienation, a state of being in which the contemplating soul is transported out of its own realm into a higher one. It is clear that within the framework of Plotinus' system, alienation is a state of being in which the soul forfeits something inferior—its separate existence—and gains something superior—submergence in the realm of the emanating One. This explains why Plotinus and his followers always characterized alienation as a state of elevation (*elevatio*), and why they never deemed it a distortion of the human realm.[4]

The same positive evaluation was featured in St. Augustine's use of the term *"alienatio."* From his introduction of the phrase *alienatio mentis a corpore* to signify the state of submergence in the divine realm,[5] it may be concluded that, like Plotinus, St. Augustine conceived of alienation as a state

[4] Plotinus, *Ennéades,* trans. Émile Bréhier (Paris: Collection des Université de France, 1924–1938), VI, pp. 1, 20, 97, *et passim.*

[5] Sancti Aurelii Augustini, *Enarrationes in Psalmos* 36, 67, in *Aurelii Augustini Opera,* X, 1, 2 (Vatican City: Typographi Brepols Editores Pontificii, 1956).

of ecstatic contemplation in which the human soul or spirit is elevated. In this use of the term, no note is taken of the negative aspect of man's being estranged from himself, or at least no negative evaluation of this aspect is implied. On the contrary, that to which reference is made is a positive state of subsistence in unity with God, a unity that requires as its cognitive means that man be transported from his own realm. This transportation from oneself according to Plotinus and St. Augustine is the necessary precondition of true contemplation because until he is alienated from himself, man remains in the realm of the deliberative and discursive intellect, a realm in which knower and known are distinguished. Since the realm of this distinction cannot be transcended without transcending the human realm, elevation, above separation and towards unity, is alienation of man from himself.

Plotinus and his followers tended to identify the state of ecstasy with the state of *theoria,* understanding by *theoria* the contemplation of spiritual essence. Why they correlated the concepts of *theoria* and *contemplatio* is a question that cannot be considered within the limits of the present discussion. It suffices to remark that in these systems, *theoria* and *alienatio* were linked in one of two ways: either *theoria* was said to require man's alienation from himself as its precondition; or *theoria,* strictly understood, was held to be identical with *alienatio* qua ecstasy.[6]

Related to this complex of ideas is the notion that to know God is to dismiss the concepts in which discursive thought is formulated, or to recognize that the conception of God consists in his non-conception. Influential in Plotinus' thought, this notion also figured in the systems of Gregory of Nyssa, Dionysius the Areopagite, and St. Bonaventure, and constituted an element both in the doctrine of negative attributes and in the doctrine of learned ignorance (*docta ignorantia*) formulated by Nicholas of Cusa. The details of the varia-

[6] *See* Ludwig Kerstiens, "Die Lehre von der theoretischen Erkenntnis in der lateinischen Tradition," *Philosophisches Jahrbuch der Görres Gesellschaft,* 66th year (Munich, 1958), pp. 380 ff.

tions on this motif need not concern us. What should be remarked is that in each variation, an attempt was made to represent a state of contemplation in which the split between knower and known exists no more. A state of being of this kind requires total alienation either from the knower or from the basic structure of his knowledge, a structure bound up with the division between knower and known. Because they identified true knowledge with the unity of knower and known, or with the unity of man and God, these systems located the realization of true knowledge beyond the limits of the human realm. This implies that identity as a cognitive ideal from man demands alienation. For by virtue of his given status, man stands outside, or even in the way, of identity.

At the heart of this position, then, a dialectical paradox arises: the paradox consists in presenting the realization of knowledge as if it subsisted beyond the ken of the knowing man; the paradox of positing an identity whose content is sustained by the total submergence of man as knower in the content, rather than by man directing himself through his intentionality toward the content as standing opposite him. The ideal of the identity brought about through the act of knowing, then, goes hand in hand with the idea of alienation. The state of identity is the positive correlative of the state of alienation. To paraphrase an observation made by Professor Gershom Scholem in connection with ecstatic Jewish mysticism, without an ideal of unity or submergence, there would be no state of alienation.[7]

DIVINE THOUGHT

An even closer relationship between the state of supreme theoretical contemplation and the state of alienation was posited by Richard St. Victor who explicitly stated that elevation of the soul occurs when the activity of divinely illuminated thought transcends the limits of human effort. He held,

[7] Gershom Scholem, *Major Trends in Jewish Mysticism* (Jerusalem: Schocken, 1941), pp. 119 ff.

moreover, that such a state of being involves the soul's alienation from itself, meaning by this a state in which the soul has eradicated its memory of objects and has undergone a transfiguration that has brought it to its present state of elevation. Neither the transfiguring process nor its culmination can be achieved by unaided human effort. According to this line of reasoning, then, alienation is a state of being that presupposes not only the self-transcendence and self-estrangement of man's soul, but also divine illumination. In other words, contact with God is not only the culmination, but also the precondition of the process of alienation. Superhuman and transhuman aid is required by the very transcendence of the separation between knower and known.[8]

The notion that in alienation man is estranged from himself in order to find himself beyond or above himself is brought into clear relief by the various shades of meaning conveyed by the concept of alienation in the contexts considered thus far. This is alienation and self-transcendence for the sake of submergence in and identification with the object. However, the object with which self-submerging conjunction and identification is sought, namely, the transcendent and divine realm, ceases to be an object once man's soul has merged with and become submerged in it.

EXTERNAL AND INTERNAL

This central implication of the classical concept of alienation underwent a radical change in the philosophy of the nineteenth century. Although Fichte used the term *"Entäusserung,"* that the terms *"Entäusserung"* and *"Entfremdung"* came into currency in the nineteenth century was largely due to the place Hegel allotted them in his system. Hence, an examination of Hegel's teaching can bring out the profound

[8] Richard St. Victor, Benjamin Major, *Patrologie Cursus Completus,* ed. J. P. Migne (Paris, 1880), CXCVI, pp. 169 ff.; Richard St. Victor (Richard of Saint Victor), *Selected Writings on Contemplation,* trans. Clare Kirchberger (London: Faber and Faber, 1957), pp. 183 ff.

change undergone by the concept of alienation, which inverts not this or that detail but the essential meaning of the classical doctrine.

To comprehend this change, some background information concerning a matter of historical interpretation is necessary. In connection with his discussion of Plotinus in his *Lectures on the History of Philosophy,* Hegel undertook to explain the concept of ecstasy and remarked that this state involves more than emotional and imaginative excitement and enthusiasm. Ecstasy, he said, requires the transcendence of sense perception. He went on to define ecstasy as pure thought subsisting by itself and sustaining itself as the object of itself.[9] That Hegel should thus interpret the key concept of the classical doctrine of ecstasy, or alienation, is very revealing. For it is clear that his interpretation no longer represented ecstasy as a state of being in which thought, or, in traditional terms, the soul, is transported out of itself, let alone a state in which the soul finds itself in a realm that transcends it. What Hegel proposed in this passage of his lecture on Plotinus was a new interpretation of ecstasy according to which the ecstatic process consists not in transcendence of discursive thought, but only in transcendence of emotional and imaginative stimulation.

The deep systematic reason for this innovation lies at the very core of Hegel's teaching. Unlike Plotinus and his followers, who proceeded on the assumption that *theoria* is realized above or beyond the limits of what may be regarded as the cognitive relation par excellence, Hegel started from the assumption that the unity of knower and known is possible within the limits of human knowledge, if that knowledge is properly understood. In other words, Hegel understood ecstasy as the subsistence of thought by itself, whereas the ancients understood ecstasy as the alienating and elevating transcendence of thought. This does not imply that Hegel was not concerned with the identity of knower and known. He was. But whereas the ancients located the realization of this identity in a tran-

[9] Hegel, *Vorlesungen über die Geschichte der Philosophie,* ed. G. J. P. J. Bolland (Leiden: A. H. Adriani, 1908), pp. 660, 665.

scendent realm beyond and above the knower, Hegel placed its realization within the knower. According to the classical doctrine, alienation is the necessary means of *attaining* transcendence to reach the known; according to Hegel, it is a means of attaining immanent enrichment of the knower.

An additional systematic factor distinguished the status of alienation in Hegel's system from the position it occupied in the contemplative system already surveyed. To understand the significance of the change Hegel introduced in the basic status of alienation, it may be contrasted with the position this concept occupied in the contemplative systems: (1) They understood alienation as a state of being in which the process of being transported out of oneself culminated, and (2) they held that in the state of alienation man discovered his true essence. By contrast, all the stages of Hegel's system at which the concept of alienation was considered are characterized by a common feature; they treated alienation as a state of division subservient to the end of unity. As a matter of principle, then, alienation was not a final state of unity for Hegel but a transitional state instrumental for the achievement of unity within, and not beyond, the limits of dialectical thought.

As early as the *Phenomenology of Spirit,* Hegel described the process whereby Spirit is rendered external to itself as the transition to existence of a spiritual essence, or—and vice versa —the return of particular individuality to what is the real essence of Spirit. Putting the matter even more pointedly, Hegel maintained that alienation will be ultimately alienated from itself and that all will return to its proper position by means of alienation. Here the change in the fundamental status of alienation is patent. In itself, alienation is a transitional state; the ultimate state is one of return, or alienation from alienation. Since it involves a distinction between man and contents, alienation cannot be presented as an ultimate state or as a state in which the end of theory is realized. Only on overcoming alienation and on bringing the world created by Spirit back into himself, does man's "self" exist. Alienation is necessary because it is a state in which (1) the objective contents of history and enlightenment are created and (2) the *"Bildung"* (shape) of man is formed by those contents. This implies, however, that alienation is but a transitional stage necessary for the unity of this formation and that its status must not exceed this intermediary condition.[10]

The same line of reasoning controls Hegel's treatment of the concept at another stage of his system, namely the philosophy of nature. At this stage, nature is described as the "other." (Its Platonic associations notwithstanding, the term "other" denotes for Hegel the estranged or foreign element of alienation.)[11] In Hegel's system, nature is the idea in the form of the being of otherness. Because it is "other" in relation to the idea, nature is external. Yet precisely as such, nature, too, is but a transitional state that can by no means be conceived as the adequate and comprehensive realization of the idea. Still, to be complete, comprehensive, and adequate to itself, the idea must include in itself the element and stage of otherness. In other words, the idea must be alienated from itself in order to return to itself.

Manifest at both stages of Hegel's system, the phenomenology of Spirit and the philosophy of nature, is the notion that the externalization of Spirit is subservient to that state of internalization in which the dialectical process of exile from Spirit finds its culmination. In Hegel's terminology, the subsistence of thought by itself—ecstasy—necessitates the diffusion of Spirit outside itself—alienation. Thus understood, alienation is not a state in which unity is realized but a state whose abolition will eventually result in the realization of unity. This implies that Hegel separated the meaning of ecstasy from the meaning of alienation.

More than this is involved, however, in the change Hegel introduced in the nature and status of alienation. Accord-

[10] Hegel, *Phänomenologie des Geistes* (Leipzig: Felix Meiner, 1921), pp. 316–322.

[11] Hegel, *Encyklopädie der philosophischen Wissenschaften,* ed. G. J. P. J. Bolland (Leiden: A. H. Adriani, 1906), p. 247, par. 92, Zusatz.

ing to the contemplative systems, alienation is a state of being in which the self-estranged soul finds itself by means of its object, God, who has ceased to be an object and has become a realm of submergence or fusion. Being a theoretical activity, contemplation discovers, but does not create, the realm of submergence. Discovery, not creation, is the essence of alienation according to the contemplative systems. Hegel, on the other hand, did not conceive of alienation as a state of being in which the Spirit is transported out of itself to discover a realm beyond itself. Alienation is creation—creation by the Spirit itself or realms such as history and nature. In the contemplative system, alienation was pure *theory,* whereas, in Hegel's system, the Spirit is tinctured with an element that might be called *poetic* (ποιητικός). The contemplative systems assumed the existence of a transcendent realm the discovery of which is the climax of theory, and the merging with which is the acme of discovery. For Hegel, transcendence in this sense does not exist. Transcendence is created, whether as nature or as history. But insofar as it does exist, created transcendence exists only in an interim manner, only until the realization of, or emergence from potentiality into actuality of total immanence, that immanence that will also include such elements as were originally alienated from one another in transcendence. Thus the systematic change in the approach to the problem of transcendence entailed a change both in the conception of theory and in the conception of alienation for theory's sake. The climax of realization was conceived by Hegel not as a departure from mind but as a return into it. Clearly, the subject of alienation in the philosophies of contemplation was the individual soul that immerses itself in the Divine One, while in Hegel's theory the subject of the process of alienation was not the single human individual, but what he called "World Spirit."

The intermediate status Hegel allotted to alienation, which creates realms outside man, and the limited status with which he invested this intermediary condition, stand out prominently at still another stage of his system, in the *Philosophy of Right.* In this, Hegel stated that man can place possessions outside himself, provided that the possessions thus placed are external by their very nature. On the other hand, those possessions that are inner determinations are not amenable to external placement; they must not be put in an alienated position and must not be forfeited or renounced in any way. In this context, Hegel made explicit reference to such possessions as belong to man's concrete and essential personality, and to the total essence of his self-consciousness. What he meant to imply was that alienation is legitimate only within the limits of merely external matters. Alienation, Hegel stated, is illegitimate when it involves man's subjection of his proper essence, as it does in slavery or in man's self-alienation from his own rationality. As examples of the latter kind of illegitimate alienation, Hegel adduced prejudice and the phenomenon of man's self-subordination to sovereign power or to authority.[12] Hegel's distinction between legitimate and illegitimate alienation, between alienation as applied to what is internal and alienation as applied to what is external, sheds reflexive light on the status of alienation in his system. This distinction reflects the pains Hegel took to prevent the application of alienation to the rationality and intellectual powers of man. The historical alienation in enlightenment or the process of learning of which he spoke in the *Phenomenology of Spirit,* exists for the sake of rationality. By means of such alienation, man's rationality is enriched and realized. Therefore, the limit of alienation lies in the fact that rationality can be subordinate neither to created objects nor to given objects. There is a palpable difference between Hegel's conception of this relation as against the view that was entertained by the proponents of the contemplative trend. Whereas the latter re-

[12] Hegel, *Grundlinien der Philosophie des Rechts* (Leipzig: Felix Meiner, 1921), pars. 65–66; Hegel, *Philosophy of Right,* trans. T. M. Knox (Oxford: The Clarendon Press, 1942), pp. 52 ff. Hans Barth traced the beginning of the idea of self-alienation to Rousseau's philosophy of culture. *See* Hans Barth, "Über die Idee der Selbstentfremdung des Menschen bei Rousseau," *Zeitschrift für philosophische Forschung* (Meisenheim am Glan, 1959), XIII, 16 ff.

garded alienation as a peak above rationality, Hegel regarded it not as a peak, but, at the most, as a course the pursuit of which fosters rationality. Behind this difference evidently stands the difference between the earlier assumption that a transcendent realm exists and Hegel's assumption that the transcendent realm of history and nature is created and that it exists only as subservient to the return into himself of the creating subject.

AMPLIFYING MIRROR

This fundamental question regarding the mode of existence of the transcendent realm and man's proper relation to that realm, affords a vantage point from which the subsequent adventures of the idea of alienation can be followed. The intrinsic line of development was in the direction of undermining, by degrees, not only the supreme status that transcendence had been allotted by the contemplative systems, but even the intermediate position in which Hegel had left it.

Alienation as creation of transcendence out of immanence was, of course, the cornerstone of Feuerbach's system. The main argument of Feuerbach was that before he discovers his essence within himself, man projects that essence beyond himself. Hence religion, or at least the Christian religion, may be defined as man's relation to himself or to his own essence, the latter seemingly being separate from man himself.

Even though Feuerbach's theory is already familiar, its fundamental aspect should be pointed out. Feuerbach's treatment of alienation in terms of creation was not analogous to Hegel's. Hegel's doctrine is concerned with the process of constituting, and consequently it ascribes constitutive power to Spirit. Hegel maintained that the process of alienation that creates the objective realm of history and the external realm of nature is real. According to Feuerbach, however, the alienated entity is imaginary, being the fabrication by man of a fictitious essence, God, and not the creation by the subject of an objective realm. In the state of alienation, man relates himself to a fictitious essence which not only does not exist but is not even created. Not real, but imaginary creation is implied by Feuerbach's assertion that man makes his essence into an object, for this object lacks even the created existence that Hegel allowed history and nature.

That in Feuerbach's teaching internalization was even more extreme than in Hegel's system is manifest in that the essence to which Feuerbach ascribed the fictitious existence of an imaginary objectivization, the divine realm, is the very essence to which the classical contemplative systems had ascribed transcendent existence par excellence. According to Hegel, alienation is a state of being in which Spirit externalizes itself for its own enrichment. For Feuerbach, alienation qua transcendence actually entailed no departure of the Spirit from itself. Hegel set a positive value on alienation to the extent that it is instrumental to Spirit. Feuerbach's reference to imaginary objectivization, rather than to directedness toward an existent realm beyond man implied a negative evaluation, if not an absolute negation, of alienation. If Feuerbach did not go so far as to negate alienation altogether, it was because he, too, regarded it as a means of man's awareness of his inner enrichment. For to Feuerbach's mind, man's conception of his essence as existing outside himself is followed by man's discovery of that essence within himself. Hence religion and its image of God serve man as a magnifying mirror, so to speak. Religion is the childish essence of man. Does not the child conceive his proper essence—the mature man—as existing beyond himself? Thus, while Hegel maintained that the realm created in and through alienation enriches its creator, Feuerbach maintained that the realm created in and through alienation educates its creator by showing him his own form and image. In seeking alienation from alienation, or the return of transcendence into immanence, Hegel sought to preserve the inner content of alienation while eliminating estrangement. Feuerbach could see no reason for maintaining the content of alienation that he regarded as totally immanent. Although the conception of this content as transcendent is, in point of fact, prior to its conception as immanent, the priority is purely temporal. From a rational point of view, it is unnecessary. In keeping with this line of reasoning, Feuerbach predicted that anthropology will replace theology, that is to say self-knowing immanence will replace its own reflections in alienation.[13]

PRACTICAL PROCESS

Yet Feuerbach did not go to the extreme of claiming that the realm created in and through alienation is a distortion of self-alienated man. Conceiving of this realm as a mirror or call, he denied it the status of a created entity, not because it distorts, but because it duplicates the human essence. He admitted, or tacitly assumed, that there is some justification for the mirror-like realm of alienation, to wit, the justification of temporal priority implicit in the historical fact that men conceive their essence as existing beyond them, before they discover it within themselves.

The extreme step of objecting to alienation on the ground that it is a distortion of man's essence was taken by Marx. Going even further than Feuerbach, Marx maintained that the realm created in alienation occupies no legitimate status whatever, not even the status of an imaginary or fictitious objectivization for the sake of human self-awareness. Alienation, Marx said, is a phenomenon confined within the limits of interhuman relations. The alien power above man can be neither the gods, nor nature, but man himself. And this alien power is erected and constituted in the process of alienation, which is not imaginary but real, that is, historical. At least, its effects in the human realm are real.

It might indeed be argued that Marx's view was not unambiguous, for he did not believe that the economic process creates a real world actually other than and alienated from the men who create that process. But Marx did maintain that men subordinate themselves to their own product, which im-

[13] Ludwig Feuerbach, "Das Wesen des Christentums," *Ludwig Feuerbach's Sämmtliche Werke,* ed. Wilhelm Bolin and Friedrich Jodl (Stuttgart: F. Frommann, 1903), VI, pp. 16, 17, 37.

poses its authortiy upon them. Moreover, in the process of alienation, the concrete, day-by-day relations between men are organized and established. In this twofold respect, the product, which indeed has no crystallization of its own, does wield real influence upon its producers. Because it is not a "heavenly" kingdom, but an "earthly" one that is created in and through alienation, the earthly product, crystallized in commodities and in economic relations, can no longer be conceived as if it were a mere fiction residing in an imaginary "heaven," as Feuerbach made it.

The practical process of alienation, then, places the product and the economic set of relations in a position of external existence over and against man as their creator. This being the case, Marx sought neither the return of the realm created in alienation into immanence, nor the discovery in this realm of an edifying image of man's internality. What he sought was to cancel the alienating and alienated determination or to abolish the relationship or estrangement that men have established between themselves and their own product. Having asserted that to abolish alienation is *ipso facto* to abolish the status of object qua object, Marx said, in a marginal comment, that this follows from Feuerbach's line of reasoning. What Feuerbach sought to abolish was obviously not the objectivity (*Gegenständlichkeit*) but the fictitious status of pseudo-objects. Purporting to be based on Feuerbach's premises, Marx's conclusion—at least with regard to the existence of the products of labor—is that the status of object qua object itself is to be abolished, since latent in its very existence is not the enrichment but the distortion of the creative subject.[14]

Thus "alienation" in Marx's system ends in the diametrical inversion of its beginning in the contemplative systems. Starting out as the idea that in being transported out of himself man accomplishes the supreme theoretical act of elevating sub-

[14] *MEGA,* I, 3, pp. 23, 24, 25, 83, 86, 90, 91, 166; Karl Marx and Friedrich Engels, *The German Ideology,* trans. and ed., with introduction, by R. Pascal (New York: International Publishers, 1947), pp. 22 ff; Bottomore, pp. 95–96, 99, 104, 105, 188.

mergence, the idea of alienation ends up as the notion that in subordination to his own product man degrades and distorts his essence. Not by submergence in a transcendent realm but by abolition of realms whose existence is estranged from man can human beings be elevated. Conceived first as elevating, then as enriching, whether in the capacity of objective contents or in the capacity of a provisional mirror, alienation finally is found to be fabricated and distorting in its very fabrication. Once defined as theory, pure and paramount, alienation is now defined as a product of practice destined to be destroyed by the very practice that produced it. Underlying the contemplative trend were two correlative tenets—(1) acknowledgment of an existent object and (2) supra-theoretical relatedness-in-alienation to that object. Underlying Marx's thought were two diametrically opposite correlative tenets—(1) nonacknowledgment of the existing object in the human realm and (2) a practical relatedness to creation of the object and to destruction of the created object. In alienation, theory found its paramount realization and practice found a product and perversion of its own creativity.

Marx's inversion of the original meaning of alienation is manifest even at the terminological style of his teaching. Even in his earlier writings, Marx called the alienated product a "fetish," the men who relate themselves to it "fetish-worshippers," and the entire relation "fetishism." [15] An object that in fact is no more than a created object and yet is illegitimately acknowledged as existing is a fetish; and alienation qua fetishism is to be abolished. Later, in *Capital,* Marx called the product or commodity a veiled thing full of metaphysical wit, adding that it has a mystical character.[16] In this description, the familiar note of Marxian irony is clearly heard. Yet

[15] *MEGA,* I, 3, pp. 107, 109, 133; Bottomore, pp. 119, 121, 148.

[16] Marx, *Das Kapital: Kritik der politischen Ökonomie* (Hamburg: O. Meissner, 1921), I, pp. 37–39; *and* Marx, *Capital: A Critical Analysis of Capitalistic Production,* trans. Samuel Moore and Edward Aveling from 3d German edn. (London: Glaisher, 1912), pp. 41 ff.

beneath the ironic surface lies an important indication of the inner logic controlling the dialectical course along which the concept of alienation developed. As conceived by the contemplative systems, alienation is indeed a state of being akin to mystical experience. It is assumed that contact with the transcendent being is attainable only by way of self-transcendence, by being transported out of oneself. The mystical character of the object with which self-submerging contact is sought, God, is unquestionable. Equally unquestionable, Marx said, is the pseudo-mystical character of the product created by alienation when it is treated as foreign and estranged by the men who created it.[17]

Thus the circle is closed, and alienation qua relatedness to transcendence becomes alienation qua human creativity and creation, as perceived in a perverted manner. The transformations undergone by this idea in its descent from a position of relatedness to the supreme transcendent existence down to a position of relatedness to human creation within the human realm may perhaps be regarded as a symptomatic manifestation of the general turn taken by the history of thought.

Taking the concept of alienation and its metamorphoses as an index of the changes that occurred in the history of European thought, we may sum up. Marx's inversion of the basic meaning of "alienation" as related to contemplation amounts to the view that human reality is totally self-enclosed, having no transcendent domain to which to relate. As such this reality is not correlated to anything transcendent, neither in terms of a reality (God) nor in terms of meanings (principles, norms). Marx assumed that practice in history up to the present creates alienation, and that the self-same practice will ultimately abolish it. Hence in his view man is totally historical. As for the historical situation as it is in the present, man is a split historical being, but he is about to become a rounded, self-

[17] The term "fetish" as used by Marx can be traced to the Latin "*facticius*" or "*factio,*" which mean "doing" or "acting." "Fetish" thus connotes the created god or else the act of attributing divine qualities to objects perceived sensuously.

identical historical being. The only way, according to Marx, to make man totally unified is to submerge him totally in the realm, or stream, of history. In other words, man is bound to go along with the course of history without an external yardstick of norms and principles to apply to it. History bears its own value criteria.

The position and the meaning of the concept "alienation" point to this implicit and explicit trend in Marx's thought. Thus the analysis of the concept of alienation can be taken as a point of departure for a criticism or a reiteration of a criticism of Marx's theory, insofar as it claims to be a philosophical theory.

INDEX